Beatrice,

It's been a great
pleasure to know
you — good luck!

love!

Food in Due Season

Daily Table Graces for the Christian Year

Compiled by David Goode

CANTERBURY
PRESS
Norwich

To my parents, Peter and Margaret

© David Goode 2005

First published in 2005 by the Canterbury Press
Norwich (a publishing imprint of Hymns Ancient &
Modern Limited, a registered charity)
9–17 St Albans Place,
London N1 0NX

www.scm-canterburypress.co.uk

British Library Cataloguing–in–Publication data

A catalogue record for this book is available
from the British Library

ISBN 1-85311-647-5

Typeset by Regent Typesetting London
Printed and bound by
Biddles Ltd, Kings Lynn, Norfolk

Contents

Foreword

Food joyfully shared is the heart of human happiness and well-being, and food shared in the context of prayer and thanksgiving is definitive of both Jewish and Christian thought and practice. For millennia Jewish identity and the Jewish faith have been sustained by the gathering of the household for the Shabbat meal, and for Christians too the central prayer takes the form of a shared meal, the Eucharist.

The prayer Jesus taught his disciples centres on the petition for 'our daily bread', and in attempting to picture the completion of human bliss and the fulfilment of all humanity's longings, the Christian imagination, like that of Jesus himself, has returned again and again to the image of the shared table: the banquet of the great king, the marriage supper of the Lamb.

All human beings must feed, but the joyful formality of a shared meal is more than mere nourishment. It is the foundation of all civilization, and it is also a reflection of the relationship between a creating God, the source of all goodness, and human beings, whose very lives depend on the earth's abundance, which though it has to be laboured for, in the end is received as a gift.

The saying or singing of grace before and after meals is therefore both a witness against the reduction of the shared meal to mere feeding, and a centring on who and what we are: simultaneously, social animals dependent on the fruits of the earth and the work of human hands, and the children of God, receiving all things from a loving Creator.

In an age of fast food and dissolving community, this beautiful book of graces invites Christian families and households to strengthen and renew their understanding of the holiness of the receiving and sharing of food.

Eamon Duffy
Professor of the History of Christianity
University of Cambridge

Acknowledgements

I am indebted to a number of people for their invaluable help with this book. It would not be possible to name them all, but I would like to record my particular thanks to Dr Peta Dunstan, our Faculty Librarian, for her unstinting support and encouragement; to Christine Smith of Canterbury Press for putting up with the late delivery of my manuscript, for her unfailing support through the production of this book, and her excellent suggestion that I research other ancient table graces in addition to those from the Breviary; to my wife, Sam, for putting up with the ridiculous turrets of mouldy old books that litter the house, and the resulting stubbed toes; and to my colleagues and fellow-members of Faculty for support they often did not even realize they were giving.

The psalm verses and canticles are from the Common Worship psalter. Quotations from the Bible are mostly from the New Revised Standard Version, or, on a few occasions, my own translations from the Greek.

Part One

Seasonal Table Graces

Introduction to the Table Graces

Not so very many years ago, it was a given fact that people said a grace before, and often after, a meal. The grace, however short, was an essential part of the meal and to pick up knife and fork and begin to eat before grace was a faux pas almost unforgivable. How times have changed. Meals are taken 'on the hoof', a sandwich grabbed here or there, food stuffed into the mouth in the shortest possible time, dinner in front of the television. I could go on, but that is enough: the fact is that we have lost the art of appreciating our food, the inestimable blessings of God in providing for us, and the benefits of eating together, having thanked him first.

Table graces were so much a part of a Christian's daily prayer life that the service book for daily prayer, the Breviary, contained them in addition to all the other services to be recited every day. The whole round of daily services is called the Daily Office, or Divine Office. The Breviary was, and still is, a compendium of prayer, containing the offices of prayer for the various hours of the day. In the first millennium, these services were recited from a number of different books, but the rise of the mendicant, or wandering, orders, such as the Franciscans, or the Order of Preachers, meant that a travelling friar could hardly carry round a dozen or more heavy volumes with him wherever he happened to wander.

So the services were shortened considerably and put into one or more volumes to make them easy to carry round. A common name for this volume was portaforium, something portable; another common name for the volume containing the abbreviated services was breviary.

These breviaries were really monastic books, designed to permit the monks and friars to say their abbreviated offices every day wherever they were. They were fairly complicated books, having a kind of skeleton of each service, the fixed parts that never vary and then many sections from which the remaining material was taken according to the celebration of the day.

Despite the commonly held misconception that piety and devotion among the lay people was practically non-existent in the medieval period, many lay people did, in fact, want a book that was similar to the Breviary for their own devotions. In the fifteenth and sixteenth centuries, suitable books were compiled, called primers, with greatly simplified offices and table graces, and these primers became hugely popular with pious layfolk.

Unfortunately, at the Reformation, the daily offices were simplified, breviaries and primers suppressed, and one of the casualties of this was the wonderful variety of table graces, which found no place in the Book of Common Prayer. So, for a number of years I have used the table graces from the excellent Anglican Breviary, a careful translation into English of Pope Pius X's Roman Breviary and other Western uses.

In its traditional place at the end of this breviary is the section 'Grace at meals', with the beautiful table blessings of the old Roman Breviary in English, and it is these short services of thanksgiving – edited to bring them into line with the popular Common Worship format and to make them conform to the Church's liturgical year as it is celebrated today, and with new, similar graces composed where the Breviary had no provision for some seasons – that form the bulk of this small book. Also included are a selection of ancient graces and blessings from the service books of other churches.

But first a few words about the structure of the table graces.

The structure of the graces

Anyone familiar with the Breviary will know that nothing in it is haphazard. Every service has a structure that hardly varies, and other parts that vary with the season and the day. The table graces are no different, though much shorter than the services for the various hours of the day.

The table graces follow the same structure every day of the year, except the last three days of Holy Week, with the verses and responses and the psalm or canticle changing with the season. The overall structure looks like this:

- An invitation, with response, to begin the grace
- A short verse or verses and response from the psalms or from other scripture
- Glory to the Father . . .
- Lord, have mercy on us . . .
- The Lord's Prayer
- Blessing of the table followed by the meal
- A short verse or a verse and response after the meal
- Prayer of thanksgiving for the meal
- A psalm or canticle, proper in the seasons
- Lord, have mercy on us . . .
- The Lord's Prayer
- A short series of verses and responses
- A blessing and the dismissal verse and response

This looks like a rather long service, but the table blessing before the meal takes a minute or two, and the short service after the meal takes three or four minutes at the most.

Notice how the meal is sandwiched in the middle of the

whole table blessing: it becomes a part of the service, a liturgical act in its own right, a way of making even a mundane necessity like taking in food an act of worship and a sort of communion with each other.

Let's look now in a little more detail at the individual parts of the structure, at what they mean and why they are there.

The invitation to bless

Table graces begin with an invitation to bless, said by the 'foremost'. This foremost is simply the most senior person: it will be a bishop, priest, monastic, householder or the most senior person at table, in that order. It is an ideal word as it carries in itself no connotation of whether that person is ordained, professed, lay, male or female, only that they are the most senior present, or the one chosen to lead the grace.

The foremost begins by calling out, in a voice loud enough to be heard by everyone: 'Make a blessing!', to which all respond: 'Make a blessing!' This invitation and the responses after the meal are particularly striking and send a message to all present that everyone, in fact, makes the blessing and not just the foremost. Even though some parts of the grace are said only by the foremost, the entire act of blessing depends on everyone's active participation from start to finish. You could also ring a bell immediately before the foremost calls out the invitation to bless, making the start of the meal even more dramatic.

During the great Fifty Days of the Easter season, the invitation to bless is replaced by the traditional Easter greeting.

The daily verse

The Apostle Paul, in his first letter to the church at Thessalonica, gives much good advice that is as valuable for us today as it was for the early Christians. One of the best-known and most pithy of his instructions to the Thessalonians is to ensure that they are always giving thanks to God:

> Give thanks in all circumstances: for this is the will of God in Christ Jesus for you. (1 Thessalonians 5.18)

Giving thanks is not just something we should do when we have received a notable gift from God, but something we should do every day and for everything. And what better way to fulfil the will of God in Christ Jesus than to give thanks every time we eat, every time we share in the blessings God has given to us in the fruits of our earth?

> Those who eat, eat in honour of the Lord, since they give thanks to God. (Romans 14.6a)

In doing this we are following the example of Christ. Every time he is recorded in the Gospels as sitting down to eat, he first gives thanks. The most poignant occasion is at the Last Supper, as Christ lay circled by his band of friends; as Paul writes,

> For I received from the Lord what I also handed on to you, that the Lord Jesus on the night that he was betrayed took a loaf of bread; and when he had given thanks, he broke it and said, 'This is my body that is for you. Do this in remembrance of me.' (1 Corinthians 11.23–24)

Each time we do the same at an everyday meal we make a remembrance of this great night, we make a spiritual communion with Christ. The Greek verb Paul uses in both the quotations above for giving thanks is *eucharisteio*, the same word from which our Eucharist, the ultimate thanksgiving, is derived.

This giving thanks before eating was standard practice in Palestine at the time of Christ, but his taking this simple act and imbuing it with the greatest significance at that last great supper resonates far beyond the four walls of that upper room.

The Evangelist Luke, in the last chapter of his gospel, tells the story of the two disciples on the road to Emmaus on Easter morning. They had heard that Christ had risen but could not quite seem to believe it. As the disciples walked the seven miles from Jerusalem to Emmaus, they talked about the events of the previous week and that morning's startling news. Luke recounts how the risen Christ joined them and walked with them, but they did not recognize him, even when he explained the scriptures to them, beginning with Moses and ending with himself.

The disciples walked and talked with Jesus without having even an inkling of who he was; he was just a knowledgeable stranger to them. As night was falling, they decided to turn in at a roadside inn and pressed the stranger to eat with them:

> When he was at table with them, he took bread, blessed and broke it, and gave it to them. Then their eyes were opened, and they recognized him; and he vanished from their sight. They said to each other, 'Were not our hearts burning within us while he was talking to us on the road, while he was opening the scriptures to us?'
>
> That same hour they got up and returned to Jerusalem; and they found the eleven and their companions gathered together. They were saying: 'The Lord has risen indeed, and he has appeared to Simon!' Then they told what had happened on the road, and how he had been made known to them in the breaking of the bread. (Luke 24.30–35)

It was only in the act of eating together, at Christ's breaking and blessing of bread, that they were able to see the risen Christ and recognize him for who he really was. And this is important for us to remember, too: we meet with and recognize the same risen Christ not only in the Eucharist, but in every meal, every fellowship, and we should have a habit of giving thanks at meals, not just for the obvious gift of food and drink, but for God's gift to us of his Christ and the Christian fellowship we share together as a result.

Getting back to the table graces, in the same way that the psalms are the backbone of the Breviary, the short psalm or scripture verses that follow the invitation are the backbone of the table graces. These verses were carefully selected for their aptness; the daily verses deal with the matter in hand, as it were: God's gracious gift of food to us.

The verse before the midday meal on days in Ordinary Time, which do not have a proper seasonal verse, is highly appropriate:

> The eyes of all wait upon you, O Lord, and you give them their food in due season: you open wide your hand, and fill all things living with plenty. (Psalm 145.16–17)

Through the year, we look to God with eager expectation that he will feed us, just as he fed the Israelites in the wilderness, Elijah in the desert, the hungry crowd on the shores of Lake Tiberias, and the disciples at the Last Supper. Everything is in its natural order, its season, and God merely has to open his hand and we are filled.

Before the evening meal, we recall that even the poor shall eat and that we who seek the Lord should praise him:

> The poor shall eat and be satisfied; they that seek after the Lord shall praise him; their hearts shall live for ever. (Psalm 22.26)

These are the verses used throughout the greater part of the year and you will soon have them committed to memory. As you can see from the digression above, these simple verses can lead to meditations on the scriptures and on the life of Christ in quite unexpected ways. They can be true food for thought in Christ's own words of rebuke to Satan:

But he answered, 'It is written, "One does not live by

bread alone, but by every word that comes from the mouth of God."' (Matthew 4.4)

The seasonal verse

At certain times in the Church's year, the daily verses are not used but are replaced by other verses, or a short combination of verse and response, calling to mind the season. In this introduction, we will briefly look at the table graces for Christmas, the Feast of the Incarnation.

> Unto us is born this day a Saviour! So let us rejoice. Sadness should find no place among those who celebrate the Birthday of Life!

So begins the sermon of Pope Leo the Great in the triumphal Matins of Christmas morning. The Saviour is born and sadness is banished. The miracle of the Incarnation also has a less obvious connection with food. The same God who simply has to open his hand to fill us with more than we can eat now takes on our flesh, our weakness, our requirement to eat to stay alive. The same God who only had to utter a word to bring the whole of creation into being, and whom even the heaven of heavens cannot contain, now cries for milk at his mother's breast.

One of the verses and responses between Christmas Day and the eve of Epiphany is taken from John the Evangelist's sublime description of Christ as the Word of God:

> The Word was made flesh, alleluia. And dwelt among us, alleluia. (cf. John 1.14)

In his great hymn in praise of his father David, King Solomon asks:

> But will God indeed reside with mortals on earth? Even heaven and the highest heaven cannot contain you, how much less this house that I have built! (2 Chronicles 6.18)

God replies in an explicit promise of the Incarnation to the prophet Ezekiel:

> My dwelling-place shall be with them; and I will be their God, and they shall be my people. (Ezekiel 37.27)

It is not until the Incarnation itself, though, that Solomon's question and God's promise to Ezekiel can be truly appreciated, until the moment when God really does dwell among us. This is powerfully recalled by one of the Angels of the Apocalypse in the Revelation to John the Divine, who repeats God's promise to Ezekiel, confirming it as an everlasting truth now that God has indeed dwelt among men:

> See, the home of God is among mortals. He shall dwell with them; they will be his peoples, and God himself will be with them. (Revelation 21.3)

John is told of the fullness of God's promise: the fulfilment of the reality of the Incarnation is made clear to him as he stands before the throne of God's glory. The true reason for, and ultimate end of, God's dwelling among men, and the redemptive power of his Christ, are revealed to John in the promise for the future to those who love and serve God:

> He will wipe every tear from their eyes. Death shall be no more; mourning and crying and pain will be no more, for the first things have passed away. (Revelation 21.4)

And then God, sitting on his throne of glory, speaks a few short words to John that contain the entire promise and its wonderful fulfilment, all the things that were foretold in the Prophets and eagerly awaited by all:

> See, I am making all things new. (Revelation 21.5)

In these few words lies the truth of the Incarnation. God spoke a perfect creation into existence by his Word, his Christ. Through the disobedience of our father Adam, the gates of Paradise were locked to us until the Christ came, until God dwelt among men. That moment was a new creation, the restoration of our rightful place as beings created in the image of God. This is the real revelation of God's purpose for us.

After both meals in the Christmas season, the verse and response declares with satisfaction that our salvation is now known: God has revealed himself to us, dwelling with us in our own flesh. It is no longer something to be foreshadowed or foretold, prophesied or awaited. It is here: God has become man that man might become God:

> The Lord has made known, alleluia. His salvation, alleluia. (cf. Psalm 98.3)

As is usual, the psalm verses end with the Gloria, the short hymn of glory to the Holy Trinity:

> Glory to the Father, and to the Son, and to the Holy Spirit; as it was in the beginning is now and shall be for ever. Amen.

I hope these brief meditations on just a couple of psalm verses that surround a meal during the Christmas season begin to show how powerful these table graces are. Just two verses, and a bit of background exploration, have taken us from the creation to the end of time, from our fall from grace to our rebirth as a new creation, once again in the image of God but this time without the possibility of tears, or death, crying or pain, for, as we speak the Christ's name Emmanuel, we say 'God is with us!'

Blessing the table

After the psalm verse of the day and the Gloria, there is a short set of prayers asking for God's mercy, and then the Lord's Prayer. It is particularly appropriate that the Lord's Prayer should be said before and after a meal:

He was praying in a certain place, and after he had finished, one of his disciples said to him, 'Lord, teach us to pray, as John taught his disciples.' He said to them, 'When you pray, say: Our Father . . .' (Luke 11.1–2a)

Whether you pray the traditional or the modern version, the message is the same: we ask for our daily bread, and tied up with this, we ask for forgiveness, not just forgiveness for ourselves, but that we might forgive others. And this forgiveness, in both directions, should be our daily bread, the staff of life.

Immediately following the Lord's Prayer is the blessing of the table, when we do as Christ did and give thanks for, and ask for his blessing on, the food before us. This blessing never changes, either during the day, or during the seasons, with the exception of Maundy Thursday, Good Friday and Holy Saturday. Notice how the blessing is first asked on us, and only then on the food itself which we obtain from God's bounty.

Thanksgiving after the meal

At the end of the meal, another verse and response are said, followed by a short prayer of thanksgiving. This prayer is followed immediately by a psalm or canticle of thanksgiving and the Gloria, the Lord's Prayer and a short series of verses and responses taken mainly from the psalms. Then there is a blessing and the dismissal responses.

Using the daily and seasonal table graces

One of Archbishop Thomas Cranmer's pet hates with the Breviary was what he describes scathingly in notes concerning the service of the Church that stand immediately after the Preface to the Book of Common Prayer:

> the manifold changings of the Service, was the cause, that to turn the Book only was so hard and intricate a matter, that many times there was more business to find out what should be read, than to read it when it was found out.

He was exaggerating, of course, but he had a point. So as not to cause the reader to suffer the same trouble, and throw out this book as Cranmer did his breviary, I have arranged the table graces in such a way that you only need one bookmark and everything is set out as it is said. This involves a certain amount of repetition, but makes the book very easy to use: on ordinary days, everything for both meals is set out in full, and on days during the seasons, everything for both meals is set out in full in the seasonal section.

Since the Breviary graces were composed, the Church has changed the way it celebrates the seasons of the liturgical year, and I have reordered some of the original Breviary provisions, and composed new table graces where they were never provided for some seasons. I have reordered, rewritten, and composed the graces in a style that will be very familiar to anyone using Common Worship.

Any lectionary or church calendar will tell you the beginning and end dates of the various seasons, and on every day that is not seasonal, the daily table graces are said.

The parts printed in normal type are designed to be said by the foremost, the parts in bold type by everyone. The psalms and canticles are said antiphonally, with everyone joining in the Gloria. The responses are obviously said as verses with their response.

Do not be afraid to adapt this if you want: I have arranged the graces so they could be said by one person alone, saying all the parts, or antiphonally as laid out, or in some other way as you choose.

Shortening the graces

Clearly not everyone will want, or be able, to use the full graces every day of the year. Grabbing a sandwich in a busy lunchtime at work and a full daily or seasonal grace are not really compatible, so you will have to use your discretion when choosing what to say and what to omit. Probably the easiest way to a quick grace is to omit everything except the blessing of the table, beginning 'Bless us, O Lord', which you can say silently over a baguette without losing time or drawing attention to yourself.

Part Two has table graces from other ancient Christian traditions, some of which are very short and easy to commit to memory. You could also use one of these when time and opportunity are short.

Part Three summarizes the main table blessing prayers from all the sources, and is an ideal way to select a quick prayer when a full grace is not possible.

You can, of course, use these other ancient graces at any time, perhaps for a bit of variety during the long period of Ordinary Time between Pentecost and Advent, at one or both meals of the day. I recommend, though, that during the seasons, you stick mainly to the seasonal graces.

Adding a little more to the graces

In an effort to make this little book appeal to the widest possible audience, I have not given any directions for using the sign of the cross, nor for the final prayer for the souls of the faithful departed that traditionally finishes any service, however short, in the Catholic tradition. This is deliberate, as it is the duty of all Christians, of whatever tradition, to give thanks to God for his gifts, and I have no intention of forcing anything from one tradition on to Christians of another tradition.

However, for those who want such directions, and the form of words traditionally used by Catholics, I give them here.

The sign of the cross is usually made over the table by the foremost in the blessing before the meal, and everyone else present usually makes the sign of the cross on themselves at the same time. You could also do the same in the prayer that follows the meal.

On Maundy Thursday, Good Friday and Holy Saturday, the graces are much more austere, and the foremost makes the sign of the cross in silence over the table before the meal and again in the prayer that follows Psalm 51 after the meal on Maundy Thursday and Good Friday, and after the canticle on Holy Saturday. Everyone present makes the sign of the cross on themselves at the same time. The end of the prayer, given in square brackets, is traditionally said silently, though it could be said aloud, either by the foremost alone or all together, if required.

Everyone also makes the sign of the cross at the blessing that begins 'The Lord bless us' after the meal. After the dismissal verse and response, it is usual for the foremost to say 'May the souls of the faithful, through the mercy of God, rest in peace', to which the reply is 'And rise in glory. Amen', and the sign of the cross is made during this prayer, too. People from the Catholic tradition often bow during the first half of the Gloria.

However, you should not feel pressured to follow these directions if you do not want to, nor be put off by the fact that some people do follow them, if they are not your cup of tea. They are optional extras, which is precisely why they have been relegated to the end of this introduction and not included in the texts themselves.

Daily Table Graces in Advent

Use these graces during Advent, which is the period from the First Sunday of Advent until Christmas Eve. I have used the short responses from the Advent antiphons and responsories in the traditional English pre-Reformation service book, the Sarum Breviary, to construct this seasonal grace, as there was never any provision in the Roman Breviary for seasonal graces in Advent.

Before the midday meal

Make a blessing!
Make a blessing!

Stir up your mighty strength, and come to our salvation
**Turn us again, O God, show the light of your countenance,
and we shall be saved** (Psalm 80.3–4)
**Glory to the Father and to the Son and to the Holy Spirit; as
it was in the beginning is now and shall be for ever. Amen**

Lord, have mercy on us
Christ, have mercy on us
Lord, have mercy on us
Our Father ...

Let us pray
Bless us, O Lord, and these your gifts, of which we are about
to partake through your bounty. Through Christ our Lord
Amen

After the midday meal

Turn us again, O God of hosts
Show the light of your countenance, and we shall be saved
(Psalm 80.7)
**Glory to the Father and to the Son and to the Holy Spirit; as
it was in the beginning is now and shall be for ever. Amen**

We give you thanks for these and for all your blessings, O
God Almighty, who lives and reigns for ever and ever
Amen
The earth is the Lord's and all that fills it, the compass of
the world and all who dwell therein

For he has founded it upon the seas and set it firm upon the rivers of the deep
Who shall ascend the hill of the Lord, or who can rise up in his holy place?
Those who have clean hands and a pure heart, who have not lifted up their soul to an idol, nor sworn an oath to a lie
They shall receive a blessing from the Lord, a just reward from the God of their salvation
Such is the company of those who seek him, of those who seek your face, O God of Jacob (Psalm 24.1–6)
Glory to the Father and to the Son and to the Holy Spirit; as it was in the beginning is now and shall be for ever. Amen

Lord, have mercy on us
Christ, have mercy on us
Lord, have mercy on us

Our Father . . .

He has given freely to the poor
And his righteousness stands fast for ever (cf. Psalm 112.9)
I shall bless the Lord at all times
His praise shall ever be in my mouth
My soul shall glory in the Lord
Let the humble hear and be glad
O magnify the Lord with me
Let us exalt his name together (Psalm 34.13)
Blessed be the name of the Lord
From this time forth for evermore (Psalm 113.2)
The Lord bless us and preserve us from all evil and bring us to everlasting life
Amen

Let us bless the Lord
Thanks be to God

Before the evening meal

Make a blessing!
Make a blessing!

For he comes, he comes to judge the earth
**With righteousness he will judge the world and the peoples
with his truth** (Psalm 96.13)
**Glory to the Father and to the Son and to the Holy Spirit; as
it was in the beginning is now and shall be for ever. Amen**

Lord, have mercy on us
Christ, have mercy on us
Lord, have mercy on us
Our Father ...

Let us pray
Bless us, O Lord, and these your gifts, of which we are about
to partake through your bounty. Through Christ our Lord
Amen

After the evening meal

For he comes to judge the earth; in righteousness shall he
judge the world
And the peoples with equity (Psalm 98.9b–10)
**Glory to the Father and to the Son and to the Holy Spirit; as
it was in the beginning is now and shall be for ever. Amen**

Blessed is the Lord in all his gifts, and holy in all his works,
who lives and reigns for ever and ever (cf. Psalm 145.18)
Amen
Give the king your judgements, O God, and your righteousness to the son of a king

**Then shall he judge your people righteously and your poor
with justice**
He shall deliver the poor that cry out, the needy and those
that have no helper
**He shall have pity on the weak and poor; he shall preserve
the lives of the needy**
He shall redeem their lives from oppression and violence,
and dear shall be their blood in his sight
**May his name remain for ever and be established as long as
the sun endures**
May all nations be blest in him and call him blessed (Psalm
72.1–2, 12–14, 17)
**Glory to the Father and to the Son and to the Holy Spirit; as
it was in the beginning is now and shall be for ever. Amen**

Lord, have mercy on us
Christ, have mercy on us
Lord, have mercy on us
Our Father ...

He has given freely to the poor
And his righteousness stands fast for ever (cf. Psalm 112.9)
I shall bless the Lord at all times
His praise shall ever be in my mouth
My soul shall glory in the Lord
Let the humble hear and be glad
O magnify the Lord with me
Let us exalt his name together (Psalm 34.13)
Blessed be the name of the Lord
From this time forth for evermore (Psalm 113.2)
The Lord bless us and preserve us from all evil and bring us
to everlasting life
Amen

Let us bless the Lord
Thanks be to God

Daily Table Graces in the Christmas Season

Use these graces during the Christmas season, which begins on Christmas Day and ends on the eve of Epiphany (5 January).

Before the midday meal

Make a blessing!
Make a blessing!

The Word was made flesh, alleluia
And dwelt among us, alleluia (John 1.14)
Glory to the Father and to the Son and to the Holy Spirit; as it was in the beginning is now and shall be for ever. Amen

Lord, have mercy on us
Christ, have mercy on us
Lord, have mercy on us
Our Father . . .

Let us pray
Bless us, O Lord, and these your gifts, of which we are about to partake through your bounty. Through Christ our Lord
Amen

After the midday meal

The Lord has made known, alleluia
His salvation, alleluia (Psalm 98.3)
Glory to the Father and to the Son and to the Holy Spirit; as it was in the beginning is now and shall be for ever. Amen

We give you thanks for these and for all your blessings, O God Almighty, who lives and reigns for ever and ever
Amen

Sing to the Lord a new song, for he has done marvellous things

His own right hand and his holy arm have won for him the victory
The Lord has made known his salvation; his deliverance has he openly shown in the sight of the nations
He has remembered his mercy and faithfulness towards the house of Israel, and all the ends of the earth have seen the salvation of our God, alleluia! (Psalm 98.1–4)
Glory to the Father and to the Son and to the Holy Spirit; as it was in the beginning is now and shall be for ever. Amen

Lord, have mercy on us
Christ, have mercy on us
Lord, have mercy on us
Our Father . . .

He has given freely to the poor
And his righteousness stands fast for ever (cf. Psalm 112.9)
I shall bless the Lord at all times
His praise shall ever be in my mouth
My soul shall glory in the Lord
Let the humble hear and be glad
O magnify the Lord with me
Let us exalt his name together (Psalm 34.13)
Blessed be the name of the Lord
From this time forth for evermore (Psalm 113.2)
The Lord bless us and preserve us from all evil and bring us to everlasting life
Amen

Let us bless the Lord
Thanks be to God

Before the evening meal

Make a blessing!
Make a blessing!

The Word was made flesh, alleluia
And dwelt among us, alleluia (John 1.14)
Glory to the Father and to the Son and to the Holy Spirit; as it was in the beginning is now and shall be for ever. Amen

Lord, have mercy on us
Christ, have mercy on us
Lord, have mercy on us
Our Father . . .

Let us pray
Bless us, O Lord, and these your gifts, of which we are about to partake through your bounty. Through Christ our Lord
Amen

After the evening meal

The Lord has made known, alleluia
His salvation, alleluia (Psalm 98.3)
Glory to the Father and to the Son and to the Holy Spirit; as it was in the beginning is now and shall be for ever. Amen

Blessed is the Lord in all his gifts, and holy in all his works, who lives and reigns for ever and ever (cf. Psalm 145.18)
Amen
Sound praises to the Lord, all the earth; break into singing and make music
Make music to the Lord with the lyre, with the lyre and the voice of melody

With trumpets and the sound of the horn sound praises before the Lord, the King
Let the sea thunder and all that fills it, the world and all that dwell upon it
Let the rivers clap their hands and let the hills ring out together before the Lord, for he comes to judge the earth
In righteousness shall he judge the world and the peoples with equity, alleluia! (Psalm 98.5–10)
Glory to the Father and to the Son and to the Holy Spirit; as it was in the beginning is now and shall be for ever. Amen

Lord, have mercy on us
Christ, have mercy on us
Lord, have mercy on us
Our Father ...

He has given freely to the poor
And his righteousness stands fast for ever (cf. Psalm 112.9)
I shall bless the Lord at all times
His praise shall ever be in my mouth
My soul shall glory in the Lord
Let the humble hear and be glad
O magnify the Lord with me
Let us exalt his name together (Psalm 34.13)
Blessed be the name of the Lord
From this time forth for evermore (Psalm 113.2)
The Lord bless us and preserve us from all evil and bring us to everlasting life
Amen

Let us bless the Lord
Thanks be to God

Daily Table Graces in the Epiphany Season

The provision in the Breviary for Epiphany and the week following concentrated only on the 'Three Wise Men' at both meals. This season, though, is really much more than that. It is a celebration of several epiphanies, or manifestations: the newborn Christ to the Wise Men; the manifestation of Christ at the beginning of his public ministry, which began with his baptism by John in the Jordan; Christ's first miracle at the beginning of this ministry, the changing of water into wine at the wedding in Cana; and his presentation in the temple on the eighth day.

As these four great manifestations of the Incarnate Christ are really aspects of one great Epiphany, the Church has restored the proper balance in celebrating them all in this season, and I have included them all in the table graces.

Use these graces during the Epiphany season, which begins on the feast of the Epiphany (6 January) and ends on the feast of the Presentation (2 February).

Before the midday meal

Make a blessing!
Make a blessing!

The kings of Tarshish and of the isles shall pay tribute; the kings of Sheba and Seba shall bring gifts, alleluia (Psalm 72.10)
The wise men saw the child with Mary his mother and they knelt down and paid him homage. Then, opening their treasure-chests, they offered him gifts of gold, frankincense, and myrrh, alleluia (cf. Matthew 2.11)
Glory to the Father and to the Son and to the Holy Spirit; as it was in the beginning is now and shall be for ever. Amen

Lord, have mercy on us
Christ, have mercy on us
Lord, have mercy on us
Our Father . . .

Let us pray
Bless us, O Lord, and these your gifts, of which we are about to partake through your bounty. Through Christ our Lord
Amen

After the midday meal

When Jesus also had been baptized and was praying, the heaven was opened, and the Holy Spirit descended upon him in bodily form like a dove, alleluia
And a voice came from heaven, 'You are my Son, the Beloved; with you I am well pleased', alleluia (Luke 3.21b–22)
Glory to the Father and to the Son and to the Holy Spirit; as it was in the beginning is now and shall be for ever. Amen
We give you thanks for these and for all your blessings, O God Almighty, who lives and reigns for ever and ever
Amen

Ascribe to the Lord, you powers of heaven, ascribe to the Lord glory and strength

Ascribe to the Lord the honour due to his name; worship the Lord in the beauty of holiness

The voice of the Lord is upon the waters; the God of glory thunders; the Lord is upon the mighty waters

The voice of the Lord is mighty in operation; the voice of the Lord is a glorious voice

The Lord sits enthroned above the water flood; the Lord sits enthroned for evermore

The Lord shall give strength to his people; the Lord shall give his people the blessing of peace, alleluia! (Psalm 29.1–4, 9–10)

Glory to the Father and to the Son and to the Holy Spirit; as it was in the beginning is now and shall be for ever. Amen

Lord, have mercy on us
Christ, have mercy on us
Lord, have mercy on us
Our Father . . .

He has given freely to the poor
And his righteousness stands fast for ever (cf. Psalm 112.9)
I shall bless the Lord at all times
His praise shall ever be in my mouth
My soul shall glory in the Lord
Let the humble hear and be glad
O magnify the Lord with me
Let us exalt his name together (Psalm 34.13)
Blessed be the name of the Lord
From this time forth for evermore (Psalm 113.2)
The Lord bless us and preserve us from all evil and bring us to everlasting life
Amen

Let us bless the Lord
Thanks be to God

Before the evening meal

Make a blessing!
Make a blessing!

Jesus changed water into wine, the first of his signs, in Cana of Galilee, and revealed his glory, alleluia
And his disciples believed in him, alleluia (cf. John 2.11)
Glory to the Father and to the Son and to the Holy Spirit; as it was in the beginning is now and shall be for ever. Amen

Lord, have mercy on us
Christ, have mercy on us
Lord, have mercy on us
Our Father . . .

Let us pray
Bless us, O Lord, and these your gifts, of which we are about to partake through your bounty. Through Christ our Lord
Amen

After the evening meal

My own eyes have seen the salvation, alleluia
Which you have prepared in the sight of all people, alleluia
(Luke 2.30–31)
Glory to the Father and to the Son and to the Holy Spirit; as it was in the beginning is now and shall be for ever. Amen
Blessed is the Lord in all his gifts, and holy in all his works, who lives and reigns for ever and ever (cf. Psalm 145.18)
Amen
How shall I repay the Lord for all the benefits he has given to me?
I will lift up the cup of salvation and call upon the name of the Lord

I will fulfil my vows to the Lord in the presence of all his people
I will offer to you a sacrifice of thanksgiving and call upon the name of the Lord
I will fulfil my vows to the Lord in the presence of all his people
In the courts of the house of the Lord, in the midst of you, O Jerusalem, alleluia! (Psalm 116.10–12, 15–17)
Glory to the Father and to the Son and to the Holy Spirit; as it was in the beginning is now and shall be for ever. Amen

Lord, have mercy on us
Christ, have mercy on us
Lord, have mercy on us
Our Father . . .

He has given freely to the poor
And his righteousness stands fast for ever (cf. Psalm 112.9)
I shall bless the Lord at all times
His praise shall ever be in my mouth
My soul shall glory in the Lord
Let the humble hear and be glad
O magnify the Lord with me
Let us exalt his name together (Psalm 34.13)
Blessed be the name of the Lord
From this time forth for evermore (Psalm 113.2)
The Lord bless us and preserve us from all evil and bring us to everlasting life
Amen

Let us bless the Lord
Thanks be to God

Daily Table Graces in Lent

Use these graces during Lent, which begins on Ash Wednesday and ends on Holy Saturday.

Lent is the Church's main penitential period. In earlier days, only one meal was eaten per day during Lent, but I have compiled graces for both the midday and evening meals, as very few people observe Lent so strictly these days.

The material selected is penitential, with the excellent Prayer of Manasseh and Psalm 51 used throughout Lent and the first few days of Holy Week. Try not to vary this material too much, and try to use at least one of the full Lenten graces every day, to keep the flavour of the season.

Note that the table graces for the last three days of Holy Week – Maundy Thursday, Good Friday and Holy Saturday – have their own special form, and are printed in the next section.

Before the midday meal

Make a blessing!
Make a blessing!

O God, according to your great goodness you have promised forgiveness for repentance
To those who have sinned against you (Prayer of Manasseh 7b)
Glory to the Father and to the Son and to the Holy Spirit; as it was in the beginning is now and shall be for ever. Amen

Lord, have mercy on us
Christ, have mercy on us
Lord, have mercy on us
Our Father . . .

Let us pray
Bless us, O Lord, and these your gifts, of which we are about to partake through your bounty. Through Christ our Lord
Amen

After the midday meal

Unworthy as we are, you will save us according to your great mercy
For all the host of heaven sings your praise, and your glory is for ever and ever (Prayer of Manasseh 14b, 15b)
Glory to the Father and to the Son and to the Holy Spirit; as it was in the beginning is now and shall be for ever. Amen
We give you thanks for these and for all your blessings, O God Almighty, who lives and reigns for ever and ever
Amen

Have mercy on me, O God, in your great goodness; according to the abundance of your compassion blot out my offences
Wash me thoroughly from my wickedness and cleanse me from my sin
For I acknowledge my faults and my sin is ever before me

Against you only have I sinned and done what is evil in your sight

So that you are justified in your sentence and righteous in your judgement

I have been wicked even from my birth, a sinner when my mother conceived me

Behold, you desire truth deep within me and shall make me understand wisdom in the depths of my heart

Purge me with hyssop and I shall be clean; wash me and I shall be whiter than snow

Make me hear of joy and gladness, that the bones you have broken may rejoice

Turn your face from my sins and blot out all my misdeeds (Psalm 51.1–10)

Glory to the Father and to the Son and to the Holy Spirit; as it was in the beginning is now and shall be for ever. Amen

Lord, have mercy on us
Christ, have mercy on us
Lord, have mercy on us
Our Father . . .

He has given freely to the poor
And his righteousness stands fast for ever (cf. Psalm 112.9)
I shall bless the Lord at all times
His praise shall ever be in my mouth
My soul shall glory in the Lord
Let the humble hear and be glad
O magnify the Lord with me
Let us exalt his name together (Psalm 34.13)
Blessed be the name of the Lord
From this time forth for evermore (Psalm 113.2)
The Lord bless us and preserve us from all evil and bring us to everlasting life
Amen

Let us bless the Lord
Thanks be to God

Before the evening meal

Make a blessing!
Make a blessing!

Turn back, you sinners, and do what is right before the Lord
Perhaps he will look with favour upon you and show you mercy (Tobit 13.6)
Glory to the Father and to the Son and to the Holy Spirit; as it was in the beginning is now and shall be for ever. Amen

Lord, have mercy on us
Christ, have mercy on us
Lord, have mercy on us
Our Father . . .

Let us pray
Bless us, O Lord, and these your gifts, of which we are about to partake through your bounty. Through Christ our Lord
Amen

After the evening meal

Hear my voice, O Lord, when I call
Have mercy upon me and answer me (Psalm 27.9)
Glory to the Father and to the Son and to the Holy Spirit; as it was in the beginning is now and shall be for ever. Amen
Blessed is the Lord in all his gifts, and holy in all his works, who lives and reigns for ever and ever (cf. Psalm 145.18)
Amen

Make me a clean heart, O God, and renew a right spirit within me
Cast me not away from your presence and take not your holy spirit from me
Give me again the joy of your salvation and sustain me with your gracious spirit
Then shall I teach your ways to the wicked and sinners shall return to you

Deliver me from my guilt, O God, the God of my salvation,
and my tongue shall sing of your righteousness

**O Lord, open my lips and my mouth shall proclaim your
praise**

For you desire no sacrifice, else I would give it; you take no
delight in burnt offerings

**The sacrifice of God is a broken spirit; a broken and contrite
heart, O God, you will not despise**

O be favourable and gracious to Zion; build up the walls
of Jerusalem

**Then you will accept sacrifices offered in righteousness, the
burnt offerings and oblations; then shall they offer up bulls
on your altar** (Psalm 51.11–20)

**Glory to the Father and to the Son and to the Holy Spirit; as
it was in the beginning is now and shall be for ever. Amen**

Lord, have mercy on us
Christ, have mercy on us
Lord, have mercy on us
Our Father . . .

He has given freely to the poor
And his righteousness stands fast for ever (cf. Psalm 112.9)
I shall bless the Lord at all times
His praise shall ever be in my mouth
My soul shall glory in the Lord
Let the humble hear and be glad
O magnify the Lord with me
Let us exalt his name together (Psalm 34.13)
Blessed be the name of the Lord
From this time forth for evermore (Psalm 113.2)
The Lord bless us and preserve us from all evil and bring us
to everlasting life
Amen

Let us bless the Lord
Thanks be to God

Daily Table Graces in Holy Week

On Monday, Tuesday and Wednesday of Holy Week, the graces are said as normal during Lent. The graces for Thursday, Friday and Saturday are terse and austere, consisting mostly of psalm verses after the meal.

The Lord's Prayer is traditionally said silently by all present on these three days; the foremost says the first two words and everyone completes the prayer in their hearts in silence. The meal is traditionally eaten in silence.

After the meal, Psalm 51 is said on Maundy Thursday, a selection of verses from Psalm 22 on Good Friday, and another selection of verses from Psalms 88, 41 and 16 on Holy Saturday.

I have departed from the Breviary provision in selecting these verses for Good Friday and Holy Saturday. Though rather dark and sombre, as befits these days, the selection that forms the canticle for Holy Saturday does end on a note of hope, anticipating the empty tomb of Easter morning and the good news of the risen Christ.

On all three days, the grace finishes with the beautiful collect for Good Friday, but without the usual ending, which makes for a stark and striking end to the meal. The meal is eaten in silence and finishes, the collect is read without an ending, and that is that.

As specified by the Breviary rubric for the end of the service of Matins and Lauds on Maundy Thursday and Good Friday, before which this meal would be eaten: 'And all arise, and depart in silence'.

MAUNDY THURSDAY

Before the meal

Christ for our sake became obedient unto death (cf. Philippians 2.8)

Our Father . . . (*The Lord's Prayer is finished silently and the meal is eaten in silence*)

After the meal

Christ for our sake became obedient unto death (cf. Philippians 2.8)

Have mercy on me, O God, in your great goodness; according to the abundance of your compassion blot out my offences

Wash me thoroughly from my wickedness and cleanse me from my sin

For I acknowledge my faults and my sin is ever before me

Against you only have I sinned and done what is evil in your sight

So that you are justified in your sentence and righteous in your judgement

I have been wicked even from my birth, a sinner when my mother conceived me

Behold, you desire truth deep within me and shall make me understand wisdom in the depths of my heart

Purge me with hyssop and I shall be clean; wash me and I shall be whiter than snow

Make me hear of joy and gladness, that the bones you have broken may rejoice

Turn your face from my sins and blot out all my misdeeds

Make me a clean heart, O God, and renew a right spirit within me

Cast me not away from your presence and take not your holy spirit from me

Give me again the joy of your salvation and sustain me with your gracious spirit

Then shall I teach your ways to the wicked and sinners shall return to you

Deliver me from my guilt, O God, the God of my salvation, and my tongue shall sing of your righteousness

O Lord, open my lips and my mouth shall proclaim your praise

For you desire no sacrifice, else I would give it; you take no delight in burnt offerings

The sacrifice of God is a broken spirit; a broken and contrite heart, O God, you will not despise

O be favourable and gracious to Zion; build up the walls of Jerusalem

Then you will accept sacrifices offered in righteousness, the burnt offerings and oblations; then shall they offer up bulls on your altar (Psalm 51)

Almighty God, we pray you to look graciously upon this your family, for whom our Lord Jesus Christ was content to be betrayed, and given up, and to suffer death on the cross

GOOD FRIDAY

Before the meal

Christ for our sake became obedient unto death
Even death upon the cross (cf. Philippians 2.8)
Our Father . . . (*The Lord's Prayer is finished silently and
the meal is eaten in silence*)

After the meal

Christ for our sake became obedient unto death
Even death upon the cross (cf. Philippians 2.8)
My God, my God, why have you forsaken me, and are so
far from my salvation, from the words of my distress?
**O my God, I cry in the daytime, but you do not answer; and
by night also, but I find no rest**
As for me, I am a worm and no man, scorned by all and
despised by the people
All who see me laugh me to scorn
They curl their lips and wag their heads, saying:
**'He trusted in the Lord; let him deliver him; let him deliver
him, if he delights in him'**
I am poured out like water; all my bones are out of joint
**My heart has become like wax melting in the depths of my
body**
My mouth is dried up like a potsherd; my tongue cleaves to
my gums; you have laid me in the dust of death
**For the hounds are all about me, the pack of evildoers close
in on me; they pierce my hands and my feet**
I can count all my bones; they stand staring and looking
upon me

They divide my garments among them; they cast lots for my clothing

Be not far from me, O Lord; you are my strength, hasten to help me

Deliver my soul from the sword, my poor life from the power of the dog (Psalm 22.1–2, 5–8, 14–20)

Almighty God, we pray you to look graciously upon this your family, for whom our Lord Jesus Christ was content to be betrayed, and given up, and to suffer death on the cross

HOLY SATURDAY

Before the meal

Christ for our sake became obedient unto death, even death upon the cross
Therefore God has highly exalted him and given him the name which is above every name (cf. Philippians 2.8–9)
Our Father (*The Lord's Prayer is finished silently and the meal is eaten in silence*)

After the meal

Christ for our sake became obedient unto death, even death upon the cross
Therefore God has highly exalted him and given him the name which is above every name (cf. Philippians 2.8–9)
My soul is full of troubles, my life draws near to the land of death
I am counted as one gone down to the Pit, I am like one that has no strength
Lost among the dead, like the slain who lie in the grave
You have laid me in the lowest pit, in a place of darkness in the abyss
My enemies speak evil about me, asking when I shall die and my name perish
All my enemies whisper together against me, against me they devise evil
Saying that a deadly thing has laid hold on me, and that I will not rise again from where I lie

Even my bosom friend, whom I trusted, who ate of my bread, has lifted up his heel against me

But you, O Lord, be merciful to me and raise me up, that I may reward them

By this I know that you favour me, that my enemy does not triumph over me

Because of my integrity you uphold me and will set me before your face for ever

Wherefore my heart is glad and my spirit rejoices; my flesh also shall rest secure

For you will not abandon my soul to Death, nor suffer your faithful one to see the Pit

Blessed be the Lord God of Israel, from everlasting to everlasting. Amen and Amen (Psalm 88.3–5, 7; 41.5, 7–12; 16.8–9; 41.13)

Almighty God, we pray you to look graciously upon this your family, for whom our Lord Jesus Christ was content to be betrayed, and given up, and to suffer death on the cross

Daily Table Graces in Easter Week

Although this great Fifty Days is all one season, which is the period from Easter Sunday until Pentecost, there is separate provision of table graces for the Paschal meal, Easter Week, from the Second Sunday of Easter until the eve of Ascension, Ascension Day itself, for the following nine days until the eve of Pentecost, and for the Day of Pentecost itself. On the Monday after Pentecost, Ordinary Time is resumed.

Use the graces in this chapter during Easter Week, which is the week from Easter Sunday until the eve of the Second Sunday of Easter.

Many churches have a Paschal meal after the Easter Vigil, usually very early on Easter morning. There is a separate provision for this meal, and it could be used at any meal on Easter Day itself, saving the other graces for Easter Week.

DURING EASTER WEEK

Before the midday meal

Alleluia, Christ is risen!
He is risen indeed, alleluia!
This is the day that the Lord has made, alleluia
Let us rejoice and be glad in it, alleluia (cf. Psalm 118.24)
**Glory to the Father and to the Son and to the Holy Spirit; as
it was in the beginning is now and shall be for ever. Amen**

Lord, have mercy on us
Christ, have mercy on us
Lord, have mercy on us
Our Father ...

Let us pray
Bless us, O Lord, and these your gifts, of which we are about
to partake through your bounty. Through Christ our Lord
Amen

After the midday meal

Alleluia, Christ is risen!
He is risen indeed, alleluia!

Blessed be the God and Father of our Lord Jesus Christ! By
his great mercy he has given us a new birth, alleluia
**Into a living hope through the resurrection of Jesus Christ
from the dead, alleluia** (1 Peter 1.3)
**Glory to the Father and to the Son and to the Holy Spirit; as
it was in the beginning is now and shall be for ever. Amen**

We give you thanks for these and for all your blessings, O God Almighty, who lives and reigns for ever and ever
Amen

O give thanks to the Lord, for he is good; his mercy endures for ever
Let Israel now proclaim, 'His mercy endures for ever'
Let the house of Aaron now proclaim, 'His mercy endures for ever'
Let those who fear the Lord proclaim, 'His mercy endures for ever'
In my constraint I called to the Lord; the Lord answered and set me free
The Lord is at my side; I will not fear; what can flesh do to me?
With the Lord at my side as my saviour, I shall see the downfall of my enemies
It is better to take refuge in the Lord than to put any confidence in flesh
It is better to take refuge in the Lord than to put any confidence in princes
All the nations encompassed me, but by the name of the Lord I drove them back
They hemmed me in, they hemmed me in on every side, but by the name of the Lord I drove them back
They swarmed about me like bees; they blazed like fire among thorns, but by the name of the Lord I drove them back
Surely, I was thrust to the brink, but the Lord came to my help
The Lord is my strength and my song, and he has become my salvation, alleluia! (Psalm 118.1–14)
Glory to the Father and to the Son and to the Holy Spirit; as it was in the beginning is now and shall be for ever. Amen

Lord, have mercy on us
Christ, have mercy on us
Lord, have mercy on us
Our Father . . .

He has given freely to the poor
And his righteousness stands fast for ever (cf. Psalm 112.9)
I shall bless the Lord at all times
His praise shall ever be in my mouth
My soul shall glory in the Lord
Let the humble hear and be glad
O magnify the Lord with me
Let us exalt his name together (Psalm 34.13)
Blessed be the name of the Lord
From this time forth for evermore (Psalm 113.2)
The Lord bless us and preserve us from all evil and bring us
to everlasting life
Amen

Let us bless the Lord, alleluia
Thanks be to God, alleluia
Alleluia, Christ is risen!
He is risen indeed, alleluia!

Before the evening meal

Alleluia, Christ is risen!
He is risen indeed, alleluia!
This is the day that the Lord has made, alleluia
Let us rejoice and be glad in it, alleluia (cf. Psalm 118.24)
**Glory to the Father and to the Son and to the Holy Spirit; as
it was in the beginning is now and shall be for ever. Amen**

Lord, have mercy on us
Christ, have mercy on us
Lord, have mercy on us
Our Father ...

Let us pray
Bless us, O Lord, and these your gifts, of which we are about
to partake through your bounty. Through Christ our Lord
Amen

After the evening meal

Alleluia, Christ is risen!
He is risen indeed, alleluia!

Through Jesus we have come to trust in God, alleluia
Who raised him from the dead and gave him glory, alleluia
(cf. 1 Peter 1.21a)
**Glory to the Father and to the Son and to the Holy Spirit; as
it was in the beginning is now and shall be for ever. Amen**
Blessed is the Lord in all his gifts, and holy in all his works,
who lives and reigns for ever and ever (cf. Psalm 145.18)
Amen

Joyful shouts of salvation sound from the tents of the
righteous

'The right hand of the Lord does mighty deeds; the right hand of the Lord raises up; the right hand of the Lord does mighty deeds'

I shall not die, but live and declare the works of the Lord

The Lord has punished me sorely, but he has not given me over to death

Open to me the gates of righteousness, that I may enter and give thanks to the Lord

This is the gate of the Lord; the righteous shall enter through it

I will give thanks to you, for you have answered me and have become my salvation

The stone which the builders rejected has become the chief cornerstone

This is the Lord's doing, and it is marvellous in our eyes

This is the day that the Lord has made; we will rejoice and be glad in it

Come, O Lord, and save us we pray. Come, Lord, send us now prosperity

Blessed is he who comes in the name of the Lord; we bless you from the house of the Lord

The Lord is God; he has given us light; link the pilgrims with cords right to the horns of the altar

You are my God and I will thank you

You are my God and I will exalt you

O give thanks to the Lord, for he is good; his mercy endures for ever, alleluia! (Psalm 118.15–29)

Glory to the Father and to the Son and to the Holy Spirit; as it was in the beginning is now and shall be for ever. Amen

Lord, have mercy on us
Christ, have mercy on us
Lord, have mercy on us
Our Father . . .

He has given freely to the poor
And his righteousness stands fast for ever (cf. Psalm 112.9)

I shall bless the Lord at all times
His praise shall ever be in my mouth
My soul shall glory in the Lord
Let the humble hear and be glad
O magnify the Lord with me
Let us exalt his name together (Psalm 34.13)
Blessed be the name of the Lord
From this time forth for evermore (Psalm 113.2)
The Lord bless us and preserve us from all evil and bring us
to everlasting life
Amen

Let us bless the Lord, alleluia
Thanks be to God, alleluia
Alleluia, Christ is risen!
He is risen indeed, alleluia!

THE PASCHAL MEAL

Before the Paschal meal

Alleluia, Christ is risen!
He is risen indeed, alleluia!

On the first day of the week, at dawn, Mary Magdalene, Joanna, Mary the mother of James and the other women came to the tomb, bringing spices and ointments to anoint the body of Christ
They found the stone rolled away from the tomb. But when they went in they did not find the body
As they stood wondering and amazed by this, suddenly two men in dazzling clothes stood beside them. The women were afraid and fell to the ground, but the men said to them:
Why do you seek the living among the dead? He is not here, but has risen, alleluia! (cf. Luke 24.1–5)
Glory to the Father and to the Son and to the Holy Spirit; as it was in the beginning is now and shall be for ever. Amen

Lord, have mercy on us
Christ, have mercy on us
Lord, have mercy on us
Our Father . . .

Let us pray
Bless us, O Lord, and these your gifts, of which we are about to partake through your bounty. Through Christ our risen Lord
Amen

Christ our passover has been sacrificed for us, alleluia!
So let us celebrate the feast, alleluia! (1 Corinthians 5.7b)

After the Paschal meal

Alleluia, Christ is risen!
He is risen indeed, alleluia!

Worthy is the Lamb that was slaughtered to receive power
and wealth and wisdom and might
And honour and glory and blessing, alleluia! (cf. Revelation
5.12)
Now have come the salvation and the power and the kingdom of our God and the authority of his Christ, for the
accuser of our brethren has been thrown down
They have conquered him by the blood of the Lamb, alleluia!
(cf. Revelation 12.10–11)
The marriage of the Lamb has come and his bride has made
herself ready
**Blessed are those who are invited to the wedding banquet of
the Lamb, alleluia!** (cf. Revelation 19.7, 9a)
**To the one who sits on the throne and to the Lamb be
blessing and honour and glory and might, for ever and ever.
Amen. Alleluia!** (cf. Revelation 5.13b)
We give you thanks for these and for all your blessings,
O God Almighty, who lives and reigns for ever and ever
Amen

O give thanks to the Lord, for he is good; his mercy endures
for ever
Let Israel now proclaim, 'His mercy endures for ever'
Let the house of Aaron now proclaim, 'His mercy endures
for ever'
**Let those who fear the Lord proclaim, 'His mercy endures
for ever'**
In my constraint I called to the Lord; the Lord answered
and set me free
**The Lord is at my side; I will not fear; what can flesh do to
me?**

With the Lord at my side as my saviour, I shall see the downfall of my enemies

It is better to take refuge in the Lord than to put any confidence in flesh

It is better to take refuge in the Lord than to put any confidence in princes

All the nations encompassed me, but by the name of the Lord I drove them back

They hemmed me in, they hemmed me in on every side, but by the name of the Lord I drove them back

They swarmed about me like bees; they blazed like fire among thorns, but by the name of the Lord I drove them back

Surely, I was thrust to the brink, but the Lord came to my help

The Lord is my strength and my song, and he has become my salvation

Joyful shouts of salvation sound from the tents of the righteous:

'The right hand of the Lord does mighty deeds; the right hand of the Lord raises up; the right hand of the Lord does mighty deeds'

I shall not die, but live and declare the works of the Lord

The Lord has punished me sorely, but he has not given me over to death

Open to me the gates of righteousness, that I may enter and give thanks to the Lord

This is the gate of the Lord; the righteous shall enter through it

I will give thanks to you, for you have answered me and have become my salvation

The stone which the builders rejected has become the chief cornerstone

This is the Lord's doing, and it is marvellous in our eyes

This is the day that the Lord has made; we will rejoice and be glad in it

Come, O Lord, and save us we pray. Come, Lord, send us now prosperity
Blessed is he who comes in the name of the Lord; we bless you from the house of the Lord
The Lord is God; he has given us light; link the pilgrims with cords right to the horns of the altar
You are my God and I will thank you
You are my God and I will exalt you
O give thanks to the Lord, for he is good; his mercy endures for ever, alleluia! (Psalm 118)
Glory to the Father and to the Son and to the Holy Spirit; as it was in the beginning is now and shall be for ever. Amen

Lord, have mercy on us
Christ, have mercy on us
Lord, have mercy on us
Our Father ...

He has given freely to the poor
And his righteousness stands fast for ever (cf. Psalm 112.9)
I shall bless the Lord at all times
His praise shall ever be in my mouth
My soul shall glory in the Lord
Let the humble hear and be glad
O magnify the Lord with me
Let us exalt his name together (Psalm 34.13)
Blessed be the name of the Lord
From this time forth for evermore (Psalm 113.2)
The risen Lord bless us and preserve us from all evil and bring us to everlasting life
Amen

Let us bless the Lord, alleluia
Thanks be to God, alleluia
Alleluia, Christ is risen!
He is risen indeed, alleluia!

Daily Table Graces from the Day after the Second Sunday of Easter until the Eve of Ascension Day

The whole life in Christ is a journey, a journey home, back to the state of perfection in which our ancestral father and mother were created, and from which they fell through disobedience.

Christ's resurrection, in itself, would not have been a particularly significant event if, like that of Jairus' daughter or Lazarus, it had been only a return to life for a certain period before death once again claimed him. We know, of course, that it so far transcended this as to be beyond our comprehension: death is trampled down not just once, for one person, for a limited time, but always, for all, and for all time.

Christ called, and still calls, us like a shepherd calling his sheep back to the fold. We are to follow him, not just through the gates of death and to new life, but further. In the same way our baptism, where we are buried with Christ and rise with him, is the start of our journey, so the Ascension, where we rise still higher with him to the heavenly places, is our goal.

Before his death, Christ spoke of rising again. Now he is risen, he speaks of ascending, and he draws us up, restores us, to become the sons and daughters of heaven we were destined to be from before our birth.

We should use these days not just to praise and glorify the risen Christ, but to prepare ourselves to rise further still, further and higher, until we reach the place which has been prepared for us since before the beginning of time, until we follow Christ all the way home, rising from death to life, and from earth to heaven.

Use these table graces from the day after the Second Sunday of Easter until the eve of Ascension Day.

Before the midday meal

Alleluia, Christ is risen!
He is risen indeed, alleluia!

Christ died for all, alleluia
So that those who live might live for him who died and was raised for them, alleluia (cf. 2 Corinthians 5.15)
Glory to the Father and to the Son and to the Holy Spirit; as it was in the beginning is now and shall be for ever. Amen

Lord, have mercy on us
Christ, have mercy on us
Lord, have mercy on us
Our Father ...

Let us pray
Bless us, O Lord, and these your gifts, of which we are about to partake through your bounty. Through Christ our Lord
Amen

After the midday meal

Alleluia, Christ is risen!
He is risen indeed, alleluia!

For as by man came death, by man has come also the resurrection of the dead, alleluia
For as in Adam all die, even so in Christ shall all be made alive, alleluia (cf. 1 Corinthians 15.21–22)
Glory to the Father and to the Son and to the Holy Spirit; as it was in the beginning is now and shall be for ever. Amen

We give you thanks for these and for all your blessings, O God Almighty, who lives and reigns for ever and ever
Amen
I will exalt you, O Lord, because you have raised me up and have not let my foes triumph over me

O Lord my God, I cried out to you and you have healed me

You brought me up, O Lord, from the dead; you restored me to life from among those that go down to the Pit

Sing to the Lord, you servants of his; give thanks to his holy name

You have turned my mourning into dancing; you have put off my sackcloth and girded me with gladness

Therefore my heart sings to you without ceasing; O Lord my God, I will give you thanks for ever, alleluia! (Psalm 30.1–4, 11–12)

Glory to the Father and to the Son and to the Holy Spirit; as it was in the beginning is now and shall be for ever. Amen

Lord, have mercy on us
Christ, have mercy on us
Lord, have mercy on us
Our Father . . .

He has given freely to the poor
And his righteousness stands fast for ever (cf. Psalm 112.9)
I shall bless the Lord at all times
His praise shall ever be in my mouth (Psalm 34.1)
My soul shall glory in the Lord
Let the humble hear and be glad
O magnify the Lord with me
Let us exalt his name together (Psalm 34.13)
Blessed be the name of the Lord
From this time forth for evermore (Psalm 113.2)
The Lord bless us and preserve us from all evil and bring us to everlasting life
Amen

Let us bless the Lord, alleluia
Thanks be to God, alleluia
Alleluia, Christ is risen!
He is risen indeed, alleluia!

Before the evening meal

Alleluia, Christ is risen!
He is risen indeed, alleluia!

Christ has risen from the dead, alleluia
The first fruits of those who have fallen asleep, alleluia
(cf. 1 Corinthians 15.20)
Glory to the Father and to the Son and to the Holy Spirit; as it was in the beginning is now and shall be for ever. Amen

Lord, have mercy on us
Christ, have mercy on us
Lord, have mercy on us
Our Father . . .

Let us pray
Bless us, O Lord, and these your gifts, of which we are about to partake through your bounty. Through Christ our Lord
Amen

After the evening meal

Alleluia, Christ is risen!
He is risen indeed, alleluia!

For since we believe that Jesus died and rose again, alleluia
Even so, through Jesus, God will bring with him those who have fallen asleep, alleluia (cf. 1 Thessalonians 4.14)
Glory to the Father and to the Son and to the Holy Spirit; as it was in the beginning is now and shall be for ever. Amen
Blessed is the Lord in all his gifts, and holy in all his works, who lives and reigns for ever and ever (cf. Psalm 145.18)
Amen

Bless the Lord, O my soul, and all that is within me bless his holy name

Bless the Lord, O my soul, and forget not all his benefits
Who forgives all your sins and heals all your infirmities
Who redeems your life from the Pit and crowns you with faithful love and compassion
The merciful goodness of the Lord is from of old and endures for ever on those who fear him; and his righteousness on children's children
On those who keep his covenant and remember his commandments to do them
Bless the Lord, all you works of his, in all places of his dominion
Bless the Lord, O my soul, alleluia! (Psalm 103.1–4, 17, 18, 22)
Glory to the Father and to the Son and to the Holy Spirit; as it was in the beginning is now and shall be for ever. Amen

Lord, have mercy on us
Christ, have mercy on us
Lord, have mercy on us
Our Father . . .

He has given freely to the poor
And his righteousness stands fast for ever (cf. Psalm 112.9)
I shall bless the Lord at all times
His praise shall ever be in my mouth
My soul shall glory in the Lord
Let the humble hear and be glad
O magnify the Lord with me
Let us exalt his name together (Psalm 34.13)
Blessed be the name of the Lord
From this time forth for evermore (Psalm 113.2)
The Lord bless us and preserve us from all evil and bring us to everlasting life
Amen

Let us bless the Lord, alleluia
Thanks be to God, alleluia
Alleluia, Christ is risen!
He is risen indeed, alleluia!

[65]

Table Graces on Ascension Day

Use these graces only on Ascension Day, before the midday meal.

Before the midday meal

Alleluia, Christ is risen!
He is risen indeed, alleluia!

I am ascending to my Father and your Father, alleluia
To my God and your God, alleluia (John 20.17)
Glory to the Father and to the Son and to the Holy Spirit; as it was in the beginning is now and shall be for ever. Amen

Lord, have mercy on us
Christ, have mercy on us
Lord, have mercy on us
Our Father . . .

Let us pray
Bless us, O Lord, and these your gifts, of which we are about to partake through your bounty. Through Christ our Lord
Amen

After the midday meal

Alleluia, Christ is risen!
He is risen indeed, alleluia!

Christ was believed in throughout the world, alleluia
And taken up in glory, alleluia (cf. 1 Timothy 3.16)
Glory to the Father and to the Son and to the Holy Spirit; as it was in the beginning is now and shall be for ever. Amen

We give you thanks for these and for all your blessings, O God Almighty, who lives and reigns for ever and ever
Amen

Let God arise and let his enemies be scattered; let those that hate him flee before him
As the smoke vanishes, so may they vanish; as wax melts at the fire, so let the wicked perish at the presence of God

But let the righteous be glad and rejoice before God; let them make merry with gladness

Sing to God, sing praises to his name; exalt him who rides on the clouds. The Lord is his name; rejoice before him!

You have gone up on high and led captivity captive; you have received tribute

Even from those who rebelled, that you may reign as Lord and God

Sing to God, you kingdoms of the earth; make music in praise of the Lord

He rides on the ancient heaven of heavens and sends forth his voice, a mighty voice

Ascribe power to God, whose splendour is over Israel, whose power is above the clouds

How terrible is God in his holy sanctuary, the God of Israel, who gives power and strength to his people. Blessed be God, alleluia! (Psalm 68.1–4, 17, 32–5)

Glory to the Father and to the Son and to the Holy Spirit; as it was in the beginning is now and shall be for ever. Amen

Lord, have mercy on us
Christ, have mercy on us
Lord, have mercy on us
Our Father . . .

He has given freely to the poor
And his righteousness stands fast for ever (cf. Psalm 112.9)
I shall bless the Lord at all times
His praise shall ever be in my mouth
My soul shall glory in the Lord
Let the humble hear and be glad
O magnify the Lord with me
Let us exalt his name together (Psalm 34.13)
Blessed be the name of the Lord
From this time forth for evermore (Psalm 113.2)
The Lord bless us and preserve us from all evil and bring us to everlasting life
Amen

Let us bless the Lord, alleluia **Thanks be to God, alleluia**
Alleluia, Christ is risen! **He is risen indeed, alleluia!**

Before the evening meal

Alleluia, Christ is risen!
He is risen indeed, alleluia!

God has gone up with a merry noise, alleluia
The Lord with the sound of the trumpet, alleluia (Psalm 47.5)
**Glory to the Father and to the Son and to the Holy Spirit; as
it was in the beginning is now and shall be for ever. Amen**

Lord, have mercy on us
Christ, have mercy on us
Lord, have mercy on us
Our Father . . .

Let us pray
Bless us, O Lord, and these your gifts, of which we are about
to partake through your bounty. Through Christ our Lord
Amen

After the evening meal

Alleluia, Christ is risen!
He is risen indeed, alleluia!

God reigns over the nations, alleluia
God has taken his seat upon his holy throne, alleluia (Psalm
47.8)
**Glory to the Father and to the Son and to the Holy Spirit; as
it was in the beginning is now and shall be for ever. Amen**

Blessed is the Lord in all his gifts, and holy in all his works,
who lives and reigns for ever and ever (cf. Psalm 145.18)
Amen

I will exalt you, O Lord, because you have raised me up and
have not let my foes triumph over me
**You brought me up, O Lord, from the dead; you restored
me to life from among those that go down to the Pit**

Exalt the Lord our God; bow down before his footstool,
for he is holy

The Lord is in his holy temple; the Lord's throne is in heaven

The Lord is king: let the earth rejoice; let the multitude of the isles be glad

Clouds and darkness are round about him; righteousness and justice are the foundations of his throne

The Lord is king: let the peoples tremble; he is enthroned above the cherubim: let the earth shake

The Lord is great in Zion and high above all peoples

Exalt the Lord our God and worship him upon his holy hill, for the Lord our God is holy

O Lord our governor, how glorious is your name in all the world, alleluia! (Psalm 30.1, 3; Psalm 99.5; Psalm 11.4; Psalm 97.1–2; Psalm 99.1–2, 9; Psalm 8.1)

Glory to the Father and to the Son and to the Holy Spirit; as it was in the beginning is now and shall be for ever. Amen

Lord, have mercy on us
Christ, have mercy on us
Lord, have mercy on us
Our Father . . .

He has given freely to the poor
And his righteousness stands fast for ever (cf. Psalm 112.9)
I shall bless the Lord at all times
His praise shall ever be in my mouth
My soul shall glory in the Lord
Let the humble hear and be glad
O magnify the Lord with me
Let us exalt his name together (Psalm 34.13)
Blessed be the name of the Lord
From this time forth for evermore (Psalm 113.2)
The Lord bless us and preserve us from all evil and bring us to everlasting life
Amen

Let us bless the Lord, alleluia
Thanks be to God, alleluia
Alleluia, Christ is risen!
He is risen indeed, alleluia!

Daily Table Graces from the Day after Ascension Day until the Eve of Pentecost

The time between Ascension and Pentecost is a time of waiting for the Church, just as it was for the disciples, a time of looking forward to the gift of the Holy Spirit. Use these graces only on these days.

Before the midday meal

Alleluia, Christ is risen!
He is risen indeed, alleluia!

A new heart I will give you, and a new Spirit I will put within you, alleluia
And I will remove from your body the heart of stone and give you a heart of flesh, alleluia (Ezekiel 36.26)
Glory to the Father and to the Son and to the Holy Spirit; as it was in the beginning is now and shall be for ever. Amen

Lord, have mercy on us
Christ, have mercy on us
Lord, have mercy on us
Our Father . . .

Let us pray
Bless us, O Lord, and these your gifts, of which we are about to partake through your bounty. Through Christ our Lord
Amen

After the midday meal

Alleluia, Christ is risen!
He is risen indeed, alleluia!

When the helper comes, whom I shall send to you from the Father, the Spirit of truth who comes from the Father, alleluia
He will testify on my behalf, alleluia (John 15.26)
Glory to the Father and to the Son and to the Holy Spirit; as it was in the beginning is now and shall be for ever. Amen

We give you thanks for these and for all your blessings,
O God Almighty, who lives and reigns for ever and ever
Amen

Make me a clean heart, O God, and renew a right Spirit
within me
**Cast me not away from your presence and take not your
Holy Spirit from me**
Give me again the joy of your salvation and sustain me with
your gracious Spirit
**Then shall I teach your ways to the wicked and sinners shall
return to you, alleluia!** (Psalm 51.10–13)
**Glory to the Father and to the Son and to the Holy Spirit; as
it was in the beginning is now and shall be for ever. Amen**

Lord, have mercy on us
Christ, have mercy on us
Lord, have mercy on us
Our Father . . .

He has given freely to the poor
And his righteousness stands fast for ever (cf. Psalm 112.9)
I shall bless the Lord at all times
His praise shall ever be in my mouth
My soul shall glory in the Lord
Let the humble hear and be glad
O magnify the Lord with me
Let us exalt his name together (Psalm 34.13)
Blessed be the name of the Lord
From this time forth for evermore (Psalm 113.2)
The Lord bless us and preserve us from all evil and bring us
to everlasting life
Amen

Let us bless the Lord, alleluia
Thanks be to God, alleluia
Alleluia, Christ is risen!
He is risen indeed, alleluia!

Before the evening meal

Alleluia, Christ is risen!
He is risen indeed, alleluia!

The helper, the Holy Spirit, whom the Father will send in
my name, alleluia
**Will teach you everything, and remind you of all that I have
said to you, alleluia** (John 14.26)
**Glory to the Father and to the Son and to the Holy Spirit; as
it was in the beginning is now and shall be for ever. Amen**

Lord, have mercy on us
Christ, have mercy on us
Lord, have mercy on us
Our Father ...

Let us pray
Bless us, O Lord, and these your gifts, of which we are about
to partake through your bounty. Through Christ our Lord
Amen

After the evening meal

Alleluia, Christ is risen!
He is risen indeed, alleluia!

When the Spirit of truth comes, alleluia
He will guide you into all the truth, alleluia (John 16.13)
**Glory to the Father and to the Son and to the Holy Spirit; as
it was in the beginning is now and shall be for ever. Amen**

Blessed is the Lord in all his gifts, and holy in all his works,
who lives and reigns for ever and ever (cf. Psalm 145.18)
Amen

You gave your good Spirit to instruct them, and you did not withhold your manna from their mouths, and gave them water for their thirst
The Spirit of God has made me
And the breath of the Almighty gives me life
I will pour out water on the thirsty land, and streams on the dry ground
I will pour my Spirit upon your descendants
And my blessing on your offspring
They shall spring up like a green tamarisk, like willows by flowing streams
In those days, I will pour out my Spirit, alleluia! (Nehemiah 9.20; Job 33.4; Isaiah 44.3–4; Joel 2.29b)
Glory to the Father and to the Son and to the Holy Spirit; as it was in the beginning is now and shall be for ever. Amen

Lord, have mercy on us
Christ, have mercy on us
Lord, have mercy on us
Our Father . . .

He has given freely to the poor
And his righteousness stands fast for ever (cf. Psalm 112.9)
I shall bless the Lord at all times
His praise shall ever be in my mouth
My soul shall glory in the Lord
Let the humble hear and be glad
O magnify the Lord with me
Let us exalt his name together (Psalm 34.13)
Blessed be the name of the Lord
From this time forth for evermore (Psalm 113.2)
The Lord bless us and preserve us from all evil and bring us to everlasting life
Amen

Let us bless the Lord, alleluia
Thanks be to God, alleluia
Alleluia, Christ is risen!
He is risen indeed, alleluia!

Table Graces on the Day of Pentecost

Use these table graces on the Day of Pentecost. On the Monday after Pentecost, Ordinary Time resumes and you should use the daily table graces for Ordinary Time until the eve of the First Sunday of Advent.

Before the midday meal

Alleluia, Christ is risen!
He is risen indeed, alleluia!

When the day of Pentecost had come, alleluia
All of them were filled with the Holy Spirit, alleluia (Acts
2.1a, 4a)
**Glory to the Father and to the Son and to the Holy Spirit; as
it was in the beginning is now and shall be for ever. Amen**

Lord, have mercy on us
Christ, have mercy on us
Lord, have mercy on us
Our Father . . .

Let us pray
Bless us, O Lord, and these your gifts, of which we are about
to partake through your bounty. Through Christ our Lord
Amen

After the midday meal

Alleluia, Christ is risen!
He is risen indeed, alleluia!

As for me, I am filled with power, alleluia
With the Spirit of the Lord, alleluia (Micah 3.8a)
**Glory to the Father and to the Son and to the Holy Spirit; as
it was in the beginning is now and shall be for ever. Amen**

We give you thanks for these and for all your blessings,
O God Almighty, who lives and reigns for ever and ever
Amen
O Lord, how manifold are your works! In wisdom you have
made them all; the earth is full of your creatures
**There is the sea, spread far and wide, and there move
creatures beyond number, both small and great**
There go the ships, and there is that Leviathan which you
have made to play in the deep

All of these look to you to give them their food in due season
When you give it them, they gather it; you open your hand and they are filled with good
When you hide your face they are troubled; when you take away their breath, they die and return again to the dust
When you send forth your Spirit, they are created, and you renew the face of the earth
May the glory of the Lord endure for ever; may the Lord rejoice in his works; he looks on the earth and it trembles; he touches the mountains and they smoke
I will sing to the Lord as long as I live
I will make music to my God while I have my being
So shall my song please him while I rejoice in the Lord
Bless the Lord, O my soul, alleluia! (Psalm 104.26–36, 37b)
Glory to the Father and to the Son and to the Holy Spirit; as it was in the beginning is now and shall be for ever. Amen

Lord, have mercy on us
Christ, have mercy on us
Lord, have mercy on us
Our Father . . .

He has given freely to the poor
And his righteousness stands fast for ever (cf. Psalm 112.9)
I shall bless the Lord at all times
His praise shall ever be in my mouth
My soul shall glory in the Lord
Let the humble hear and be glad
O magnify the Lord with me
Let us exalt his name together (Psalm 34.13)
Blessed be the name of the Lord
From this time forth for evermore (Psalm 113.2)
The Lord bless us and preserve us from all evil and bring us to everlasting life
Amen

Let us bless the Lord, alleluia **Thanks be to God, alleluia**
Alleluia, Christ is risen! **He is risen indeed, alleluia!**

Before the evening meal

Alleluia, Christ is risen!
He is risen indeed, alleluia!

The Spirit of the Lord God is upon me, alleluia
Because the Lord has anointed me, alleluia (Isaiah 61.1)
**Glory to the Father and to the Son and to the Holy Spirit; as
it was in the beginning is now and shall be for ever. Amen**

Lord, have mercy on us
Christ, have mercy on us
Lord, have mercy on us
Our Father ...

Let us pray
Bless us, O Lord, and these your gifts, of which we are about
to partake through your bounty. Through Christ our Lord
Amen

After the evening meal

Alleluia, Christ is risen!
He is risen indeed, alleluia!

God's love has been poured into our hearts, alleluia
Through the Holy Spirit that has been given to us, alleluia
(Romans 5.5)
**Glory to the Father and to the Son and to the Holy Spirit; as
it was in the beginning is now and shall be for ever. Amen**

Blessed is the Lord in all his gifts, and holy in all his works,
who lives and reigns for ever and ever (cf. Psalm 145.18)
Amen

O Lord, you have searched me out and known me; you
know my sitting down and my rising up; you discern my
thoughts from afar
**You encompass me behind and before and lay your hand
upon me**

Where can I go then from your Spirit? Or where can I flee from your presence?

If I climb up to heaven you are there; if I make the grave my bed, you are there also

If I take the wings of the morning and dwell in the uttermost parts of the sea

Even there your right hand shall lead me, your right hand hold me fast

How deep are your counsels to me, O God! How great is the sum of them!

If I count them, they are more in number than the sand, and at the end, I am still in your presence, alleluia! (Psalm 139.1, 4, 6–9, 17–18)

Glory to the Father and to the Son and to the Holy Spirit; as it was in the beginning is now and shall be for ever. Amen

Lord, have mercy on us
Christ, have mercy on us
Lord, have mercy on us
Our Father . . .

He has given freely to the poor
And his righteousness stands fast for ever (cf. Psalm 112.9)
I shall bless the Lord at all times
His praise shall ever be in my mouth
My soul shall glory in the Lord
Let the humble hear and be glad
O magnify the Lord with me
Let us exalt his name together (Psalm 34.13)
Blessed be the name of the Lord
From this time forth for evermore (Psalm 113.2)
The Lord bless us and preserve us from all evil and bring us to everlasting life
Amen

Let us bless the Lord, alleluia
Thanks be to God, alleluia
Alleluia, Christ is risen!
He is risen indeed, alleluia!

[83]

Daily Table Graces in Ordinary Time

Use these graces during Ordinary Time, which is the period from the day after the feast of the Presentation of Christ (or the Monday after the nearest Sunday, if the feast is being kept on that Sunday) until Shrove Tuesday, and the period between the day after Pentecost and the eve of the First Sunday of Advent.

This last period of Ordinary Time is rather long, so feel free to experiment with the graces from other ancient sources in Part Two, especially on weekdays. Do not be afraid of variety: you don't eat the same meal every day, so try some of the other graces if you find the daily graces are getting a bit boring.

Before the midday meal

Make a blessing!
Make a blessing!

The eyes of all wait upon you, O Lord, and you give them their food in due season: you open wide your hand, and fill all things living with plenty (Psalm 145.16–17)
Glory to the Father and to the Son and to the Holy Spirit; as it was in the beginning is now and shall be for ever. Amen

Lord, have mercy on us
Christ, have mercy on us
Lord, have mercy on us
Our Father . . .

Let us pray
Bless us, O Lord, and these your gifts, of which we are about to partake through your bounty. Through Christ our Lord
Amen

After the midday meal

All your works praise you, O Lord
And your faithful servants bless you (Psalm 145.11)
Glory to the Father and to the Son and to the Holy Spirit; as it was in the beginning is now and shall be for ever. Amen

We give you thanks for these and for all your blessings, O God Almighty, who lives and reigns for ever and ever
Amen

O praise the Lord, all you nations, praise him, all you peoples

**For great is his steadfast love towards us, and the faithful-
ness of the Lord endures for ever** (Psalm 117)
**Glory to the Father and to the Son and to the Holy Spirit; as
it was in the beginning is now and shall be for ever. Amen**

Lord, have mercy on us
Christ, have mercy on us
Lord, have mercy on us
Our Father . . .

He has given freely to the poor
And his righteousness stands fast for ever (cf. Psalm 112.9)
I shall bless the Lord at all times
His praise shall ever be in my mouth
My soul shall glory in the Lord
Let the humble hear and be glad
O magnify the Lord with me
Let us exalt his name together (Psalm 34.13)
Blessed be the name of the Lord
From this time forth for evermore (Psalm 113.2)
The Lord bless us and preserve us from all evil and bring us
to everlasting life
Amen

Let us bless the Lord
Thanks be to God

Before the evening meal

Make a blessing!
Make a blessing!

The poor shall eat and be satisfied: they that seek after the Lord shall praise him: their hearts shall live for ever. (Psalm 22.26)
Glory to the Father and to the Son and to the Holy Spirit; as it was in the beginning is now and shall be for ever. Amen

Lord, have mercy on us
Christ, have mercy on us
Lord, have mercy on us
Our Father . . .

Let us pray
Bless us, O Lord, and these your gifts, of which we are about to partake through your bounty. Through Christ our Lord
Amen

After the evening meal

The Lord appointed a memorial for his marvellous deeds; the Lord is gracious and full of compassion
He gave food to those who feared him; he is ever mindful of his covenant (Psalm 111.4–5)
Glory to the Father and to the Son and to the Holy Spirit; as it was in the beginning is now and shall be for ever. Amen

Blessed is the Lord in all his gifts, and holy in all his works, who lives and reigns for ever and ever (cf. Psalm 145.18)
Amen

O praise the Lord, all you nations, praise him, all you peoples
For great is his steadfast love towards us, and the faithfulness of the Lord endures for ever (Psalm 117)
Glory to the Father and to the Son and to the Holy Spirit; as it was in the beginning is now and shall be for ever. Amen

Lord, have mercy on us
Christ, have mercy on us
Lord, have mercy on us
Our Father . . .

He has given freely to the poor
And his righteousness stands fast for ever (cf. Psalm 112.9)
I shall bless the Lord at all times
His praise shall ever be in my mouth
My soul shall glory in the Lord
Let the humble hear and be glad
O magnify the Lord with me
Let us exalt his name together (Psalm 34.1–3)
Blessed be the name of the Lord
From this time forth for evermore (Psalm 113.2)
The Lord bless us and preserve us from all evil and bring us to everlasting life
Amen

Let us bless the Lord
Thanks be to God

Part Two

Other Ancient Table Graces

Introduction

In the course of researching this book, I collected and read an enormous quantity of source material. And, in that inimitable way that research has of turning up the most interesting things in what look like the least interesting places, my search for the oldest Christian table grace brought me an unexpectedly pleasant surprise: I found it in the latest of all the sources I used.

In this section is a selection of table graces from the almost unimaginable austerity of the third-century monks of the Egyptian desert to the almost equally unimaginable opulence of the court of Queen Elizabeth I in sixteenth-century London.

The unlikely connection between these two places and periods was, as I said, a source of considerable surprise to me: it was in an Elizabethan primer that I found what is probably the oldest known Christian table grace, composed by Egyptian monks in their desert cells.

How ironic that the same prayer may have been used by the Desert Fathers to bless their frugal meals as was used to bless huge tables, groaning with every kind of luxurious food, at the court of Good Queen Bess.

An Egyptian Monastic Table Grace

I first found this prayer in an 1870 edition of The Primer, *printed by Joseph Masters of London. This little book is edited from a number of Elizabethan printed primers, and the editor, given only as 'GM', noted in the introduction that the text of this grace was taken by the primer compilers from one of the sermons on the Gospel according to St Matthew by St John Chrysostom, the fifth-century Patriarch of Constantinople.*

John Chrysostom was a popular teacher and his sermons are very useful for understanding how the scriptures were interpreted by the early Church Fathers. His surname is really a nickname, meaning 'golden-mouthed', from his elegant and eloquent preaching.

Chrysostom lived in the second half of the fourth century, from AD *347 to 407, and this prayer was already ancient in his day. Commenting on the sixteenth chapter of Matthew, Chrysostom reminds his listeners of how the Egyptian monks have taken literally Christ's words:*

If anyone desires to come after me, let him deny himself, and take up his cross, and follow me. (Matthew 16.24)

The monks left everything behind to take on a life of austerity and spiritual warfare against the Enemy. Chrysostom praises the monks for what they have done, and is particularly taken by the table grace they use after what must to us have been a very frugal meal:

I praise and admire the monks that have occupied the desert places, as for the rest, so for this saying. For after having had their breakfast, or rather after dinner (for breakfast they do not have at any time, because they know that the present time is one of mourning and fasting); after dinner then, in saying certain hymns of thanksgiving to God, they make mention of this expression also.

And if you would like to hear the very hymns themselves, that you too may say them continually, I will rehearse to you the whole of that sacred song. The words of it then stand as follows:

'Blessed God, who feeds me from my youth up, who gives food to all flesh: fill our hearts with joy and gladness, that always having all sufficiency we may abound in every good work in Christ Jesus our Lord; with whom to you be glory, honour and might, with the Holy Spirit, forever. Amen.

'Glory to you, O Lord; glory to you, O Holy One; glory to you, O King; that you have given us food to make us glad. Fill us with the Holy Spirit, that we may be found well-pleasing before you, not being ashamed, when you give to every man according to his works.'

Now this whole hymn is worthy of admiration, but especially the ending of it. That is, because meals and food often dissipate and weigh us down, the monks put this saying as a kind of bridle on the soul at the time of indulgence, reminding it of the time of judgement.

Considering that Chrysostom encourages his hearers to use this prayer 'continually', and bearing in mind the tremendous influence he had on the development of the Byzantine church, it is perhaps surprising that another set of prayers and not this one became the table graces used by the Orthodox churches. (The table graces used by the modern Orthodox churches are given later in this part.)

This short grace, the most ancient Christian grace we

know, is a perfect way to vary the daily graces, especially during Ordinary Time. It is only two paragraphs long and easily committed to memory. Follow Chrysostom's advice and make use of it.

For convenience, what follows is the table grace, extracted from Chrysostom's sermon, for use after a meal.

After a meal

Blessed God, who feeds me from my youth up, who gives food to all flesh: fill our hearts with joy and gladness, that always having all sufficiency we may abound in every good work in Christ Jesus our Lord; with whom to you be glory, honour and might, with the Holy Spirit, forever

Amen

Glory to you, O Lord; glory to you, O Holy One; glory to you, O King; that you have given us food to make us glad. Fill us with the Holy Spirit, that we may be found well-pleasing before you, not being ashamed, when you give to every man according to his works.

Amen

Another Egyptian Table Grace

After the Council of Chalcedon, in AD *451, the Egyptian church split over the question of the two natures of Christ. Those who rejected the Council's seminal definition:*

> *We teach . . . one and the same Christ, Son, Lord, Only-begotten, known in two natures, without confusion, without change, without division, without separation . . .*

are known as non-Chalcedonians, and the Church of Egypt, or Coptic Church as it is known, fell out of communion with those churches which did accept this definition of the two natures of Christ.

The following table grace, used before the meal, is used by the Coptic Church and a version of it is found in most current editions of Ti Agpeya, *the Book of Hours or Breviary.*

This delightful grace could be used at either a midday or evening meal, during Ordinary Time, as an alternative. Note how Psalm 145.16–17, familiar from the grace before the midday meal during Ordinary Time, is paraphrased at the beginning of the prayer.

Before a meal

Blessed are you, O Lord, who supported us from our youth and granted to us your blessings, and prepared food for every creature; for the eyes of all wait on you, you who gave them their food in due season. You open your hands and fill all living things.

To you is due glory, praise, blessing and thanksgiving for the food that you have prepared for us. Stretch forth your right hand and bless this food set before us for the nourishment of our bodies. Let it be for power and health of our lives.

Grant salvation, grace, blessing and purity to all those who partake of it. Lift our minds to you at all times to seek our spiritual and eternal food. Grant that we may labour for the everlasting food which is for life eternal.

Grant us to be partakers of your evening banquet. Grant us the food of blessing, the cup of salvation, and fill our hearts with joy. Grant us a peaceful life, joy of the soul and health of the body.

Teach us to seek your pleasure in all things so that when eating, drinking or labouring, we do it all for the glory of your holy name. For yours is the glory for ever and ever
Amen

An Armenian Table Grace

Another of the non-Chalcedonian churches, the Church of Armenia, has the distinction of being the first established church in the world. While persecution raged in the Roman Empire under Diocletian at the end of the third century, St Gregory the Illuminator was converting and baptizing King Trdat of Armenia. Trdat then declared Christianity the state religion of Armenia, decades before Constantine the Great first tolerated Christianity and eventually made it the religion of the Roman Empire.

This version of the Armenian table graces was originally given in Rituale Armenorum, translated by Conybeare and Maclean and published in Oxford in 1905. Conybeare used a late-thirteenth-century manuscript for the part of the breviary in which the graces are found, but there is no reason to doubt that they are quite ancient prayers, though probably with some additions to what would have been a simpler original grace.

As these table graces are quite long, and similar in format (but not in content) to the graces in the first section of this book, I have put them into the same style. Conybeare and Maclean's translation is in rather archaic English, so I have edited it, and used the Common Worship psalter for quotations from the psalms. There is an instruction written on the manuscript after the initial verses from Psalm 145 which says 'all antiphonally', so there is no doubt that these graces were used by the Armenian Church in this very familiar way.

It is of great interest that the Egyptian monastic grace above, from the sermons of John Chrysostom, makes its appearance in the Armenian grace, though padded out with a considerable amount of what is probably later material.

This Armenian grace makes a perfect alternative if you feel the graces in Part One are getting a bit tedious.

Before the meal

The eyes of all wait upon you, O Lord, and you give them their food in due season: you open wide your hand, and fill all things living with plenty (Psalm 145.16–17)
Glory to the Father and to the Son and to the Holy Spirit; as it was in the beginning is now and shall be for ever. Amen

Merciful and compassionate is the Lord
He gives food to them that fear him
Let us pray to Almighty God to bestow on us the food of gladness, and to replenish our hearts out of the fullness of his creatures
Almighty Lord our God, give us life and have mercy
Bless, O Christ our God, with spiritual blessings the food and drink of your servants, and vouchsafe health of soul and body, to the end that by indulging with religious sobriety our bodily needs, we may become, together with your saints, sharers of your blessings that do not fade away, and of your kingdom of heaven. And with thankfulness, let us glorify you with the Father and the all-holy Spirit, now and ever
Amen
Our Father . . .

Lord Jesus, we are filled with your blessings
Let us give thanks to the Lord our God

The eyes of the Lord are upon them that fear him and have trust in his mercy

To save their souls from death, and to feed them in time of hunger

Our souls wait patiently on the Lord

For he is our helper and defender

In him shall our hearts be glad, and in his holy name we will trust

Let your mercy, O Lord, be upon us, as we have hoped in you

Glory to the Father . . .

Glory to you, O Lord, who feeds us and makes us glad

Christ, who replenishes us, we give you thanks

Let us give thanks for the plenteous gifts of the Lord our God, who feeds us day by day in abundance in his loving-kindness. To the end that he may make us his servants, according as we wait and hope, partakers of his spiritual riches and of the kingdom of heaven.

Almighty Lord our God, give us life and have mercy

After the meal

Blessed are you, Lord our God, who feeds us from childhood

And gives food to all beings of flesh and blood

Fill our hearts with joy and gladness, that we may continually have sufficiency of all things, in Christ Jesus our Lord, to whom is due glory, honour and might, with the Holy Spirit, for ever

Amen

Glory to you, O Lord

Glory to you, O God

Glory to you, O Christ, king of glory, who has given us

the food of gladness, and has filled our hearts out of the fullness of your all-sufficing mercy: replenish us with your Holy Spirit, so that we may win approval before you and may not be ashamed. For you come to reward each man according to his works. And to you is due glory, honour and might, with the Holy Spirit, for ever

Amen

May God bless those that eat. May he bestow the reward of his goodness on all workers and benefactors, and bless them all. May the fullness of this table last undiminished and unfailing. To Christ our God who has fed us be glory, for ever and ever

Amen

Let this table be blessed in the name of God, Father, Son, and Holy Spirit, for ever and ever

Amen

In every hour let us give praise and thanks and glory to Father, Son and Holy Spirit

To Christ our God, who feeds us and makes us rejoice, and consoles us, be glory for ever and ever. Amen

The Orthodox Table Graces

As noted earlier, the modern Orthodox churches do not, as I noted above, use the preferred grace of John Chrysostom, but the graces following. I have arranged them to be said responsorially, as in Part One, and use the Common Worship psalter for psalm quotations and the familiar form of the Gloria.

In some ways these are similar to the Breviary graces, though with very different prayers. It is unusual that there are no psalm verses, either before or after the midday meal.

These graces can be used as a complete replacement for those given in Part One on any day during Ordinary Time.

Before the midday meal

Our Father . . .
Glory to the Father and to the Son and to the Holy Spirit; as it was in the beginning is now and shall be for ever. Amen

Lord have mercy, Lord have mercy, Lord have mercy
O Christ our God, bless the food and drink of us your servants, for you are holy, now and for ever, and to the ages of ages
Amen

After the midday meal

We thank you, O Christ our God, that you have filled us with your earthly blessings. Do not deprive us also of your heavenly kingdom, but as you came in the midst of your disciples and gave them peace, come also among us and save us
Glory to the Father and to the Son and to the Holy Spirit; as it was in the beginning is now and shall be for ever. Amen

Lord have mercy, Lord have mercy, Lord have mercy
Blessed is God who has mercy and nourishes us from his abundant gifts, by his grace and love for mankind, always, now and for ever, and to the ages of ages
Amen

After the evening meal

The poor shall eat and be satisfied: they that seek after the Lord shall praise him: their hearts shall live for ever (Psalm 22.26)

Glory to the Father and to the Son and to the Holy Spirit; as it was in the beginning is now and shall be for ever. Amen

Lord have mercy, Lord have mercy, Lord have mercy
O Christ our God, bless the food and drink of us your servants, for you are holy, now and for ever, and to the ages of ages

Amen

For you, Lord, have made me glad by your acts and I sing aloud at the works of your hands. Lord, lift up the light of your countenance upon us

You have put gladness in my heart, more than when their corn and wine and oil increase

In peace I will lie down and sleep

for it is you Lord, only, who make me dwell in safety (Psalms 92.4; Psalm 4.6b-8)

Glory to the Father and to the Son and to the Holy Spirit; as it was in the beginning is now and shall be for ever. Amen

Lord have mercy, Lord have mercy, Lord have mercy
God is with us, he that has mercy and nourishes us by his grace and love for mankind, always, now and for ever, and to the ages of ages

Amen

Table Graces from the English Primers

As I noted at the beginning of Part Two, I found what is probably the most ancient known Christian table grace in an Elizabethan primer. There are also table graces in two primers issued a few years earlier, during the reign of Henry VIII.

In 1539, shortly after his death, the primer of John Hilsey, Bishop of Rochester, was published on Cromwell's orders, and contains a short set of table graces. I have edited them slightly for language and, as above, used the Common Worship psalter for psalm verses.

A fuller set of graces is found in what is called King Henry's Primer, 'set forth by the King's Majesty and his clergy to be learned and read, and none other to be used throughout all his dominions' in 1545. These table graces are clearly based on the graces from the Roman Breviary, but have some interesting prayers and blessings not found in the Latin breviaries.

From Bishop Hilsey's Primer

Before dinner

The eyes of all wait upon you, O Lord, and you give them their food in due season: you open wide your hand, and fill all things living with plenty (Psalm 145.16–17)
Our Father . . .
O Lord God our heavenly Father, bless us, and these gifts we receive from your blessing and bounteous goodness, through your Son Jesus Christ
Amen

After dinner

We thank you, O Lord our Father, by your Son Jesus Christ our Lord, for all your benefits, who is alive and reigns from age to age, world without end
Amen

Before supper

Christ, who at the Last Supper gave himself to us, promising his body to be crucified and his blood to be shed for our sins, bless us and our supper
Amen

After supper

Honour and praise be to God the King everlasting, immortal, invisible and only wise, for ever and ever
Amen

God almighty, Father of all mercy, and God of all consolation, give us grace to consent together in the knowledge
of your truth, through Jesus Christ, that we may with one
mind and one mouth glorify God the Father of our Lord
Jesus Christ
Amen

From King Henry's Primer

Before dinner

The eyes of all wait upon you, O Lord, and you give them their food in due season: you open wide your hand, and fill all things living with plenty (Psalm 145.16–17)
Good Lord, bless us, and all your gifts which we receive from your bounteous goodness, through Christ our Lord
Amen

The king of eternal glory make us partakers of his heavenly table
Amen

God is love, and he that abides in love abides in God, and God abides in him (1 John 4.16). God grant us all to dwell with him
Amen

After dinner

The God of peace and love promise always to dwell with us
And you, Lord, have mercy on us
Glory, honour and praise be to you, O God, who has fed us from our tender age
And gives sustenance to every living thing
Replenish our hearts with joy and gladness that we, always having sufficient, may be rich and plentiful in all good works, through our Lord Jesus Christ
Amen

Lord, have mercy on us
Christ, have mercy on us
Lord, have mercy on us
Our Father ...
Lord, hear my prayer

And let my cry come before you (cf. Psalm 39.13)
From the fiery darts of the Devil, both in times of well-being
and in adversity (weal and woe), may our Saviour Christ be
our defence, buckler and shield (cf. Psalm 91.4–5)
Amen

God save the Church, the Queen, the country, and God
have mercy on all Christian souls
Amen

Before supper

O Lord Jesus Christ, without whom nothing is sweet nor
savoury, we beseech you to bless our supper, and with your
blessed presence to cheer our hearts, that in all our meats
and drinks we may taste and savour of you to your honour
and glory
Amen

After supper

Blessed is God in all his gifts
And holy in all his works (cf. Psalm 145.18)
Our help is in the name of the Lord
who has made heaven and earth (cf. Psalm 124.7)
Blessed be the name of the Lord
From this time forth for evermore (Psalm 113.2)
Most mighty Lord and merciful Father, we give you hearty
thanks for our bodily sustenance, requiring also most
entirely your gracious goodness, so to feed us with the
food of your heavenly grace, that we may worthily glorify
your holy name in this life, and after be partakers of the life
everlasting, through Christ our Lord
Amen

God save the Church, the Queen, the country, and God
have mercy on all Christian souls
Amen

Part Three

Short Table Graces

Introduction

There will be many occasions on which it is not possible to use the full table graces: at work, in a restaurant, at a friend's house for dinner, etc. This section condenses the main blessing prayers from the graces into a form that offers a very brief single prayer to use when time is short, or the circumstances are not favourable to the full grace. The origin of each prayer showsis given in brackets.

Short Table Graces

Choose any one of these prayers before and after any quick meal.

Before a meal

Bless us, O Lord, and these your gifts, of which we are about to partake through your bounty. Through Christ our Lord. Amen. (Roman Breviary, English and other Western service books) To you is due glory, praise, blessing and thanksgiving for the food that you have prepared for us. Stretch forth your right hand and bless this food set before us for the nourishment of our bodies. Let it be for power and health of our lives. Amen. (Coptic (Egyptian) Book of Hours)

Bless, O Christ our God, with spiritual blessings the food and drink of your servants, and vouchsafe health of soul and body, to the end that by indulging with religious sobriety our bodily needs, we may become, together with your saints, sharers of your blessings that do not fade away, and of your kingdom of heaven. And with thankfulness, let us glorify you with the Father and the all-holy Spirit, now and ever. Amen. (Armenian service books)

Let us give thanks for the plenteous gifts of the Lord our God, who feeds us day by day in abundance in his loving-kindness. To the end that he may make us his servants, according as we wait and hope, partakers of his spiritual riches and of the kingdom of heaven. Amen. (Armenian service books)

O Christ our God, bless the food and drink of us your servants, for you are holy, now and for ever, and to the ages of ages. Amen. (Modern Eastern Orthodox service books)

O Lord God our heavenly Father, bless us, and these gifts we receive from your blessing and bounteous goodness, through your Son Jesus Christ. Amen. (Bishop Hilsey's English Primer)

Christ, who at the Last Supper gave himself to us, promising his body to be crucified and his blood to be shed for our sins, bless us and our supper. Amen. (Bishop Hilsey's English Primer)

Good Lord, bless us, and all your gifts which we receive from your bounteous goodness, through Christ our Lord. Amen. (King Henry VIII's English Primer)

O Lord Jesus Christ, without whom nothing is sweet nor savoury, we beseech you to bless our supper, and with your blessed presence to cheer our hearts, that in all our meats and drinks we may taste and savour of you to your honour and glory. Amen. (King Henry VIII's English Primer)

After a meal

We give you thanks for these and for all your blessings, O God Almighty, who lives and reigns for ever and ever. Amen. (Roman Breviary, English and other Western service books)

Blessed is the Lord in all his gifts, and holy in all his works, who lives and reigns for ever and ever. Amen. (Roman Breviary, English and other Western service books)

Blessed God, who feeds me from my youth up, who gives food to all flesh; fill our hearts with joy and gladness, that always having all sufficiency we may abound in every good work in Christ Jesus our Lord; with whom to you be glory, honour and might, with the Holy Spirit, forever. Amen. (Egyptian monastic blessing)

Glory to you, O Christ, king of glory, who has given us the food of gladness, and has filled our hearts out of the fullness of your all-sufficing mercy: replenish us with your Holy Spirit, so that we may win approval before you and may not be ashamed. For you come to reward each man according to his works. And to you is due glory, honour and might, with the Holy Spirit, for ever. Amen. (Armenian service books)

May God bless those that eat. May he bestow the reward of his goodness on all workers and benefactors, and bless them all. May the fullness of this table last undiminished and unfailing. To Christ our God who has fed us be glory, for ever and ever. Amen. (Armenian service books)

Let this table be blessed in the name of God, Father, Son, and Holy Spirit, for ever and ever. Amen. (Armenian service books)

Blessed is God who has mercy and nourishes us from his abundant gifts, by his grace and love for mankind, always, now and for ever, and to the ages of ages. Amen. (Modern Eastern Orthodox service books)

We thank you, O Lord our Father, by your Son Jesus Christ our Lord, for all your benefits, who is alive and reigns from age to age, world without end. Amen. (Bishop Hilsey's English Primer)

God almighty, Father of all mercy, and God of all consolation, give us grace to consent together in the knowledge of your truth, through Jesus Christ, that we may with one mind and one mouth glorify God the Father of our Lord Jesus Christ. Amen. (Bishop Hilsey's English Primer)

Replenish our hearts with joy and gladness that we, always having sufficient, may be rich and plentiful in all good works, through our Lord Jesus Christ. Amen. (King Henry VIII's English Primer)

Most mighty Lord and merciful Father, we give you hearty thanks for our bodily sustenance, requiring also most entirely your gracious goodness, so to feed us with the food of your heavenly grace, that we may worthily glorify your holy name in this life, and after be partakers of the life ever-lasting, through Christ our Lord. Amen. (King Henry VIII's English Primer)